The Nature of the Game

Roland H. Koller II

Aspen Publications
839 South 250 West
Orem, Utah 84057

THE NATURE OF THE GAME

 For information address Aspen Publications, 839 South 250 West, Orem, Utah, 84057.

International Standard Book Number: 0-9603756-1-9

Library of Congress Catalog Card Number: 79-56602

What This Book Is About

The book you are about to read is a labor of love. It was originally written to my children in the hope that the principles it contains would help them live lives which were more meaningful and satisfying than they would otherwise have been. To the extent that they do so, the book will prove to be of inestimable worth, both to me and to them.

As what follows suggests, I truly feel that this is one of the most important books that they or anyone else will ever read. It contains what I consider to be the wisdom of economics. Actually, I would have given it that title were it not for the fact that the word economics often tends to frighten off readers who consider the subject difficult to understand. As I hope to show in the pages which follow, however, nothing could be further from the truth. This book is written so as to frighten off no one, for the principles it contains are valuable to all.

As you may already have guessed, I am an economist. The longer I have taught economics, however, the more apparent it has become to me that the economics profession has failed rather miserably to make its subject useful to the average person. Books on economics tend to be abstract, mathematically-oriented, and, most important of all, to deal for the most part with topics in which the average person is only marginally interested. This is a tragedy. It is a tragedy because the subject of economics contains a veritable treasure house of wisdom. Furthermore, it is wisdom which is intensely **practical** in nature and which is of **everyday practical importance** to every single person alive. This book is an effort to remedy this situation. In it are contained those portions of economic theory which I believe to be **genuinely useful to the average individual** in solving the most important problem that he or she will ever face—how to make the most of their lives. It is the sort of book which I truly wish someone had given me years ago, had required that I read it, and had also required that I understand it. The principles it contains are obtained by most of us only through the course of long (and often sad) experience, and many of these principles are never really grasped at all. And yet, an understanding of these principles could prevent so many, many problems for each of us. What this book contains is, in essence, a "world view", a way of thinking about the world in which you spend each and every day, a framework, if you will, for understanding economic life and for understanding it in a way which will really **help** you as you pursue your goals within it. Since what is really important in life is not so much what we accomplish as how we view what we accomplish, the possession of such a world view is of inestimable value.

It would be my hope that this book would become somewhat of a reference book to those who possess it. It was purposely kept very short in hopes that they would read it, that they would reread it occasionally, and that they would review parts of it whenever a really important economic decision had to be made. I would hope, in other words, that they would use it as a guide to help them avoid some of the snares and pitfalls of economic life. If the book will serve this purpose, I will consider its creation the most rewarding and worthwhile thing I have ever done.

TO MY CHILDREN

(Not dedicated to them,

written to them)

Economics is not something that one "does". It is something that one "understands". Understanding it, however, he then does the things that he does "do" differently.

TABLE OF CONTENTS

A Word of Advice

This book was not meant to be read rapidly.

The material it contains is often highly concentrated, and unless one approaches it slowly and thoughtfully a good deal of its meaning may be lost.

It was also not meant to be browsed.

The economic process is something which must be understood in its entirety if it is really to be understood at all. The reader who reads only bits and pieces of this book will not only fail to obtain the value that is in it, **he may actually mislead himself as a result.** This applies especially to the material in Part II, which should be read completely, and in its proper sequence, if anything like its full value is to be obtained.

Part I

Your Economic Problem

Of all the great and profound truths you may learn in this life, none is more true nor more profoundly significant than this: **You have an economic problem.**

Today, as you read this page, you possess a set of assets. This set is composed as follows. First, there are your physical characteristics and capabilities. These include such things as how tall you are, how fast you can run, how well you can see, how attractive you are to the opposite sex, and how healthy you are. Next, you possess a set of skills and knowledge, that is, a set of things you know and things you know how to do. Third, you have a set of mental capabilities. Included here would be such things as how well you are able to carry out abstract reasoning, how well you can remember, and how fast you can read. Then there is your personality. You have a personality that is unlike that of any other person in the world. It is a personality that some people find attractive and others find less so. It is one of your assets. Next, you have a set of associates. You have a set of people whom you know and who know you, and you have a specific relationship with each one of them. Each of these people is in a position to either help you or hurt you in some very specific ways. Sixth, you have a particular social standing. That is, by virtue of such things as who you are, who your parents are, and the social class you belong to, you have a specific amount of prestige, a certain ability to command respect, which is quite apart from your actual accomplishments and abilities. Next, you have an imagination. You have a certain amount of creativity. You have a certain ability to visualize things in ways other than they currently are—to discover new ways of doing old things or new things to do with old methods. Eighth, you have an outlook on life. This is the way you view yourself, your experiences, your purpose in living, your personal worth, and the like. It encompasses both your self-image and your religion.

Thus far, we have only considered one category of your assets, those which are very much a part of yourself. But there are also others. Your ninth group of assets consists of those things which you possess—your property. These include such things as the money you have in your checking account, your home, any other real estate you may own, your car, your toothbrush, any securities you may possess such as corporate bonds or common stocks, any businesses you may own, and the shirt on your back. Finally, asset number ten is your time. You have exactly 24 hours each day for the rest of your life.

Along with your assets, you have desires. These desires include all the things you would like to do, all the things you would like to have, all the places you would like to go, and all the things you would like to experience. Your desires are peculiar to you. They arise from who can say what sources. All that can be said about them with certainty is that their satisfaction is beyond your grasp.

The great truth, and the basis of all your problems, is this: **Your assets are insufficient to provide you with the satisfaction of your desires.**

Think about that statement for a moment, for it is profound. Your assets are **insufficient** to provide you with the satisfaction of your desires. You will be able to satisfy some of your desires. You will be able to attain some of your goals. But there is simply no way for you to attain them all.

Surely, you may think, your desires are not so immense that no conceivable amount of wealth would enable you to satisfy them. But your desires are not fixed. As you gain in assets, they will expand. Should you get a better job, for example, your new associates will have greater possessions than your old ones had, and this will make you less satisfied. Even if you are somehow impervious to the new horizons associated with increased wealth, your time will prove insufficient to do all that you would like. Or your health will not permit it. Or something else will constrain you. If this is not the case, there is no point in your reading any further for you not only have no economic problem, you have no problems at all. For the remainder of you, however, you to whom this book is relevant, read on.

Inasmuch as your assets are insufficient to enable you to satisfy all of your desires, you must decide which of them will go unfulfilled. To decide which is the problem you face. It is your economic problem.

Your problem is thus to determine how to use your assets so as to attain the most satisfaction you possibly can, that is, to get the very most out of life. It is a simple problem of allocation. You must allocate your assets. That is, you must earmark them for specific uses in such a way as to maximize a certain objective, your own satisfaction or happiness.

Two elements are required in order to solve this problem. First, you must understand precisely what it is you want, and, second, you must make an explicit, conscious effort to solve it. You thus have two tasks. First, you must decide what you want out of life. Second, you must decide what you **really** want out of life by stating explicitly the things you are willing to do without. This could very possibly be the most important thing you ever do.

Solving Your Economic Problem

How do you actually do this? How do you actually solve your economic problem so as to get a maximum of satisfaction from your life? One way to do it is as follows.

First of all, you should sit down, pick up a pencil, and write a general statement about what you want to do with the rest of your life.

Why the rest of your life? Isn't that a little extreme? Surely, you may think, the distant future is so uncertain that such a statement would be an exercise in futility. If you think this, however, you are wrong. You must include the rest of your life for a very simple reason--it is simply impossible to rationally do otherwise. You cannot plan for the future in little blocks. You can't even plan how to spend tomorrow without some expectation about what you will be doing the next day.

Furthermore, is your future really all that uncertain? You can very easily estimate how long you will live. Unless you have some particularly unusual health condition, an estimate can be obtained from a publication entitled **Vital Statistics of the United States** which is put out annually by the U.S. Public Health Service. If you were a white female and were 35 years old in 1976, for example, it says that your life expectancy at that time was 44.2 more years. As for what you would like to do with this time, you must have some idea. As you grow and gain experience, your views on this will no doubt evolve, but that is certainly no reason why you should not try and state those views as they exist right now. What this book is about is making the most of your life, and unless you have some idea of what you want to do with that life, there is not a chance in this world that you will accomplish this. Consequently, if you can't even write a general statement of your goals in life, you should stop right now and think about it until you can.

After you have written your general goals, you should next try to translate them into something a little more specific. Your view of what you would like to do with your life implies some rather specific requirements. You will, for example, have to eat. You will have to sleep. You will need a wardrobe of some sort. Unless you plan to live in the wilderness, you will probably want some type of automobile. You will also need to live in some type of dwelling. If you desire a large family, you will have to provide certain things for them. In other words, your general aims in life imply a lot of rather specific requirements, and the next step in the solution to your problem is to make these requirements explicit to the very best of your ability.

Again, this may seem like a difficult task, especially if you are young and inexperienced. Fortunately, it is not necessary for you to state these requirements precisely. Rough estimates will do just fine at this point, and they are all that can really be expected anyway.

Having reached this point in the solution to your economic problem, you will have a document which states as nearly as you can currently forecast those items which you will need to acquire and those things you will need to accomplish in order to achieve the goals you have set for yourself in life. Your next step is to estimate the cost of each of these, both in terms of time and in terms of money. Again, a rough estimate is all that can be hoped for, but such an estimate is all that is required.

After you have made an estimate of the expenditures of time and money which you feel will be necessary for you to reach your goal, your next step is to estimate how much of these two assets you will have available. The time estimate is easy. You will have 24 hours a day from now until the date on which you estimate you are going to die. The estimate as to the amount of money you will have available is more complex, however, and requires some explanation.

Where will the money come from? It will come from other people. They will give it to you either in return for some service you have performed for them, out of the goodness of their hearts, or because the law requires them to do so. We will consider these in turn.

If other people give money to you in return for a service it will be because of a service which was provided them by one of the assets which you possess. It will be in return, for example, for your letting them use a piece of your land, letting them use some of your money for a certain period of time, or letting them command the use of a piece of your time. Consequently, the income you can expect to receive from this source will be determined by the set of assets which you currently possess and the way you are able to transform this set of assets into another set in the future. Consequently, the way to estimate your stream of future income is to take each of your assets in turn and estimate the amount that you feel other people will be willing to pay for the service that that asset can perform in the most valuable use to which it can be put. Then you simply add these estimates up over all of your assets.

In estimating your future income it is useful, I believe, to make a distinction between those of your assets which have value to you in and of themselves and those which do not. Time, for example, can be used directly while money must be exchanged for something else which you can use directly to satisfy your desires. Similarly, your home can be used directly while the government bonds you may own cannot. For convenience, we will label assets of the former group, that is, those assets which yield you services directly, as Type I assets and assets of the latter group as Type II assets. The distinction is not clear-cut, especially since it may well be argued that the possession of any asset helps satisfy one's desire for security in an uncertain world, but I believe it is a useful one to make.

The estimation process then proceeds as follows. First take each of your Type II assets in turn and estimate the income stream that it will produce in the best use to which you can think of putting it. If you had a piece of land, for example, which you felt you could rent out for X dollars per year (and if this was the best use of that piece of land that you could think of), then your income stream from that source would be X dollars per year for each year that it was rented out minus any taxes or other expenses which you would have to pay in order to continue receiving the rent. Second, you simply add up these income streams over all of your Type II assets.

In addition to money which you will receive in return for service to others, you may very well receive money for other reasons as well. This would include any money you receive from charitable organizations and any money you receive through a governmental income-redistribution program. An example of the first would be flood relief provided by the Red Cross, and examples of the second would include rent subsidies, social security benefits, and unemployment compensation. You should estimate the income stream you will receive from each of these sources (net, of course, of what it will cost you to receive them).

When you have completed all the steps thus far considered, you will have two sets of estimates: One an estimate of the expenditures, by year, of time and money which you feel will be required in order to achieve your specified goal in life and the other an estimate, again by year, of the amount of time and money income (from government, from charity, and from your Type II assets) which you will have available to cover these expenditures. The next step is straightforward: You compare the two estimates.

In order to compare your estimates of available time and money with the expenditures of time and money which you feel will be required to achieve your goals in life, you should proceed as follows.

First, take a fresh sheet of paper and on it write five columns of numbers, Columns M1 through M5. In the first column, simply list all the years included in the period in which you have an interest, that is, the period including the life expectancies of all those persons who will have a voice in the final solution you adopt. In the second column, write down for each of these years the total money expenditures which you have already estimated will be required during that year to achieve the goals you have selected. In Column M3 write down your estimate of the money income you will receive each year from your Type II assets, from charity, and from government. In the fourth column, write the difference between column three and column two, that is, the figure in M3 minus the figure in M2. Finally, make Column M5 a cumulative total of the figures in Column M4 plus the stock of available "money and near money" which you possess at the present time. This stock will include your current holdings of cash, the current balance of your checking account, and the current balance of your savings account minus the amount you wish to retain in these categories as a reserve against unforeseen circumstances. (For reasons which will be explained in Part II, economists frequently refer to the first two of these, that is, to cash and checking account balances, as "money" and to savings account balances as "near money." This explains the curious title for Column M5.) Note that since your stock of money and near-money will fluctuate through time, any income which you expect to receive from that source must be adjusted to reflect this fluctuation. Finally, label the sheet of paper "Feasibility Analysis, Part I: Money." Your sheet of paper should now appear as follows, where E is used to denote expenditures, I is used to denote income, S is used to denote the stock of available money and near-money, and the subscripts indicate the years to which the figures apply (1 indicating the present year).

Feasibility Analysis Part I: Money

(M1) Year	(M2) Estimated Expenditures	(M3) Estimated Income	(M4) Difference	(M5) Estimated Stock of Available Money & Near Money
Present year	E_1	I_1	$I_1 - E_1$	Present Stock $= S_1$
Next year	E_2	I_2	$I_2 - E_2$	$S_2 = S_1 + I_1 - E_1$
The next year	E_3	I_3	$I_3 - E_3$	$S_3 = S_2 + I_2 - E_2$
.	.	.	.	.
.	.	.	.	.
.	.	.	.	.
Last year in which you have an interest	E_n	I_n	$I_n - E_n$	$S_n = S_{n-1} + I_{n-1} - E_{n-1}$

Let's take an example. Assume the year to be 1980, and assume that Mr. Jones has made the following estimates of his money expenditures over the remainder of his life.

Year	Food	Clothing	Travel	Rent	Medical	Total
1980	$10	$ 5	$ 0	$10	$5	$30
1981	10	10	25	10	5	60
1982	10	15	0	10	5	40
1983	10	5	25	10	5	55
1984	10	5	0	10	5	30
1985	10	10	35	10	10	75
1986	10	10	0	10	10	40
1987	10	5	25	10	10	60
1988	10	5	0	10	10	35
1989	10	5	25	10	10	60

Also assume that his estimated income stream is as follows.

Year	Income
1980	$50
1981	50
1982	50
1983	30
1984	30
1985	30
1986	30
1987	30
1988	30
1989	30

Finally, assume that Mr. Jones currently has $10 in his checking account and $270 in his savings account and that he wishes to maintain a minimum of $50 in his savings account as a reserve against the unexpected.

Mr. Jones' feasibility analysis for money would then appear as follows (where it has been assumed for simplicity that he expects to derive no income from his stock of money and near-money).

Feasibility Analysis, Part I: Money

(M1)	(M2)	(M3)	(M4)	(M5)
Year	Estimated Expenditures	Estimated Income	Difference	Estimated Stock of Available Money & Near-Money
1980	$30	$50	$20	$230
1981	60	50	-10	250
1982	40	50	10	240
1983	55	30	-25	250
1984	30	30	0	225
1985	75	30	-45	225
1986	40	30	-10	180
1987	60	30	-30	170
1988	35	30	- 5	140
1989	60	30	-30	135
				105

Now take a second sheet of paper and on it write four columns of numbers, Columns T1 through T4. In the first column, list the same years as you did in Column M1. In the second column, write the total expenditure of time which you have estimated will be necessary during each year in order to meet your goals. In Column T3, write the number of hours which will be available during each year. This will be 8760 hours each year for each person included in your plan (8784 for leap years) minus whatever number of hours you feel you would like to retain as "slack" to allow for unforeseen circumstances. In the fourth column, write the difference between column three and column two, that is the figure in T3 minus the figure in T2. You will not need a fifth column in this case because time cannot be accumulated. You either spend it as it comes or it is gone forever. Finally, label this sheet of paper "Feasibility Analysis, Part II: Time."

Now consider Column M5, the fifth column on your money worksheet, and Column T4, the fourth column on your time worksheet. Are any of the figures in these two columns negative? A negative figure anywhere in either of these columns indicates that your goals probably cannot be met (as stated) from government, charity, or your Type II assets. A negative figure in T4 means that you plan to use more time than you will probably have available. A negative figure in M5 means that the day will very likely come when you will be unable to pay your bills. Hence, you must alter your plans in such a way as to remove all negative figures from Columns T4 and M5, and you must do so in what you consider to be the most painless possible way. To do this is to solve your economic problem.

The solution to your problem is conceptually very simple. Its importance lies in the fact that what you will be doing as you solve it is deciding what you want out of life. I mean deciding what you **really** want out of life by specifying those items which you choose to do without. This is not something which should be done casually.

A good first step in reaching your solution is to try and rearrange your money income and expenditure streams so as to remove the negative figures from column M5. This can be done in essentially two ways: you may borrow money or you may sell off Type II assets. In the first case, you should seek to ascertain the sort of loans you might be able to obtain and adjust column M2 accordingly. If, for example, you had originally planned to spend $5,000 for a boat in 1981 but decided instead to pay for it in monthly installments over a 5-year period, you would subtract $5,000 from the 1981 figure in Column M2 and then increase the entries in that column for 1981-1985 to reflect the repayment of the loan. In the second case, you should estimate the amount you could obtain by selling various of your Type II assets and adjust Column M3 accordingly. For example, if you decided to sell a bond in 1983 and expected to receive $1,000 for it, you should increase the figure in Column M3 for 1983 by $1,000 and then decrease the figures in Column M3 for 1983 and all subsequent years to reflect the absence of the interest income from the bond you sold. (It should be noted, incidentally, that the receipts obtained by selling a Type II asset have been treated here as "income" merely to keep the procedure as simple as possible. In reality, of course, such receipts are not income at all since their expenditure would constitute a depletion of one's stock of assets. So long, however, as one bears in mind the fact that to spend such receipts is to deplete one's stock of assets, it is perfectly permissible to treat them in the manner explained here. To be consistent, of course, one should then treat the purchase of a Type II asset as a negative entry in Column M3.)

If financial manipulations such as these are sufficient to remove all of the negative values from Column M5, and if there are no negative values in Column T4, you are fortunate indeed. This is not ordinarily the case, however. Usually some negative values remain in M5. If so, then the significance of this to you is that charity, government, and your Type II assets alone will not enable you to achieve your goals in life. You must, therefore, turn to assets of Type I to remove these negative values. You must obtain money income by selling the services of assets such as your car, your house, and your time, assets which provide satisfactions to you just as they stand. Obtaining money income in this way involves a sacrifice. You are unable to enjoy the use of an asset the services of which you sell to another individual. This being the case, you must decide if the additional money that a given Type I asset will bring on the market is sufficient to justify the loss of satisfaction which the sale of its services implies. You must, in other words, decide which you would rather have, the use of the asset itself or the things you could obtain with the money which the sale of its services would provide. In terms of your worksheet, this means that you must decide which expenditures to remove from Columns M2 and T2 in order to make the numbers in Columns M5 and T4 nonnegative. (Inasmuch as the surrender for money of the use of any Type I asset other than time is equivalent to spending less money on it, the two acts may be treated the same way insofar as your worksheets are concerned. That is, both of them may be treated as reductions in the expenditure figures in Column M2.)

One of the most fundamental lessons of economics is that nothing is free, that everything has a cost. This cost is whatever must be sacrificed in order to enjoy it. As you solve your economic problem, you will become well aware of this fact. If you elect, for example, to sell some of your time in return for a salary, you do not simply add the extra money received to Column M3. You must also add the extra time expended to Column T2. Since the items in Column T4 cannot be negative, this means that you must forego other expenditures of your time in order to take the job. This is a very genuine sacrifice and must be considered when you are deciding how much of your time to trade for money. If you plan to work 40 hours per week, for example, there will be forty less hours available each week for sleep, study, fishing, travel, or whatever else you can think of to spend your time on. Consequently, you will want to transfer a unit of time from your own use to the disposal of others only if the items which the resulting income will purchase hold greater value to you (after considering the satisfaction which you derive from the work itself) than the items which must be sacrificed in order to produce the income. Following this rule, then, removing the expenditures of your choice from Columns M2 and T2 until no more negative figures appear in either Column M5 or T4, but transferring control of your Type I assets to other individuals only if the expected satisfaction from doing so exceeds the sacrifice involved, will bring you to the solution to your economic problem. Furthermore, it will bring you to the complete solution to your problem. This is because it will lead you not only to place the right amount of each of your assets at the disposal of other people, it will also specify the people at whose disposal to place them.

When you are through, you will have decided not only how you plan to spend your time and money during each future period, but also such matters as what occupation to select, where to invest your savings, and what to do with those six acres in Montana that you inherited from your Aunt Bessie. You will also have decided something else.

Obviously, the less time you have to place at the disposal of others to obtain any given future item, the lower the required sacrifice will be, and the better off you will be. You must, therefore, use your time in such a way as to produce as much income per period of time as possible (again, considering the satisfaction which you obtain from doing the work itself). But what is your time worth to other people? This depends upon the other assets which we considered earlier, namely, your skills, your knowledge, your capabilities, your personality, and the like. Consequently, placing your time in those occupations where it will produce the greatest income requires that you take measures to transform your current set of assets into a set which will make your time as valuable as possible. You will, therefore, employ your time and money not only in personal consumption or in serving others directly, but in self-improvement as well. You will invest a certain amount in yourself, in making your own time more valuable, both to yourself and to others. The amount you devote to this purpose will, of course, depend upon what you must sacrifice in order to do it and upon the difference in your assets which you expect it to make.

When you have reached this point, when you have placed each of your assets in the specific use in which you believe it will contribute the very most toward the satisfaction of your desires and have decided how to use the time and income stream which you will then have available, you will have solved your economic problem. You will not be blissful. You will not have reached Nirvana. But you will have done the best you can. You will still be limited by your assets, but you will have explicitly thought through your problem and you will have solved it. You will know that you are using whatever assets you possess in the very best way you know how. You will not have peered into the future and observed your destiny, however. The future is uncertain. The actual events of the rest of your life are going to depend upon your current set of assets, what you do with those assets, and just plain luck. Consequently, you could end up the richest person in the world or the poorest, and nothing that is written in this book should reduce the excitement or the suspense of your coming battles in the slightest way. What you **will** have seen, however, is what you believe your future is **most likely** to be like, and it is my belief that if you have made a conscientious attempt to be both thorough and accurate in applying the procedure outlined here this view will be of no small value to you as you proceed through life.

Having solved your economic problem, there are two more things which you will need to do in order to keep it solved. The first of these is to write up your lifetime budget. This is simply a piece of paper on which you record the way in which you have already chosen to use your time and your money during each future year. There is no new decision-making involved here. Compiling it is simply a clerical job. But it is well worth the time it takes.

As you proceed along in life, you are going to be exposed to many demands upon your time and your money. Indeed, the very essence of your economic problem is that you won't have enough of these to go around. There will thus be a constant stream of things coming up which seem urgent and which seem to require some of your assets. There will thus be a very strong tendency to forget what you have done up to this point, that is, to ignore the solution to your economic problem, to ignore your true objectives, to lose sight of the forest because of the trees, and to get less out of life than you otherwise could have done. Hence, the need for the lifetime budget. This document will serve you for years to come as a constant reminder of how you chose to use your assets when you really took the time to think it through. It will protect you as much as is possible from taking ill-considered actions which will not be in your own best interest **as you yourself perceived that interest when you really took the time to do so.** Your lifetime budget will serve you much like a written constitution, causing you to think twice before you use your assets in ways which are very different from those which it specifies.

This comment brings me to the last thing you must do if you are to really solve your problem in a meaningful sense. You must periodically update your solution.

The future is inherently uncertain, and your initial solution is based upon nothing more than your current expectations as to what the future will be like. As time passes, you will gain new information about your goals in life, about the income which your assets are actually capable of producing, and about a great many other things which are relevant to your solution. Consequently, you should periodically take the time to revise your solution to reflect this new information. Certain revisions, such as adding a new item to your budget or deciding which items to delete as a consequence of an unexpected reduction in your expected income stream, will be easy to make. Others, such as adjusting for significant changes in the prices which you face, may be more burdensome. Consequently, you probably ought to try to make minor revisions once each year and go through a thorough update every four or five years. Needless to say, you should make at least a minor revision any time you contemplate making a major expenditure of either time or money which is not included in your lifetime budget.

If you have proceeded according to the advice given thus far, you will be able to answer a very important question, a question which very few people can answer intelligently, namely, whether or not you can "afford" something. Whenever someone considers a new purchase, the only meaningful question he should ask himself is whether he would rather have the proposed item or the items which must be sacrificed in order to make available the time and money necessary to obtain it. The only way, in other words, to really tell if you want to acquire something is to compare the satisfactions it offers with what an economist would refer to as its "opportunity cost," namely, those satisfactions which you must sacrifice in order to obtain it. Most people make this decision with only the foggiest notion of what the opportunity cost of, say, a snowmobile really is. This is because, never having taken the time to do what is suggested above, their planning horizons are unnecessarily limited. Never having actually **written down** their expectations about their future needs and resources, never having **stated explicitly** the assumptions upon which those expectations are based, they are subject to the shifting sands of pessimism and optimism, of courage and despair, and they cannot really feel good about their decision even if the decision happens to be correct. You, however, should be able to see more accurately what an item will cost you in terms of the other types of consumption which you might have enjoyed, and you will feel much more satisfied with the decision which you ultimately make. Your answer will not be precise (precision in such matters being impossible), but it will be a great deal more precise than it would have been had you not gone through the process described above.

An Illustration: Solving My Own Economic Problem

We have now completed our discussion about how you can solve your economic problem. Hopefully, the process has been described clearly enough to enable you to proceed, but there may still be a certain skepticism on your part as to whether or not the process we have described is actually workable. Even if you are not a skeptic, an example is always welcome. Consequently, I will now relate my experience in solving my own economic problem. The only things I will not be relating are the actual time and dollar magnitudes involved. This deletion is simply a matter of privacy, and I would advise you to do the same if you ever relate your experience with this procedure to others. To show someone the actual figures is to reveal more about yourself than it is wise to do.

Some years ago, my wife and I attended a party. The party was held at the home of some friends of ours, a beautiful place in one of the nicer sections of the small town in which we live. As we drove home, we were depressed. So far as we knew, our friends had an income which was similar to ours, and yet when we contrasted the home in which we had just been entertained with the one to which we were returning, we couldn't help wondering whether we were really getting the most out of life.

Both of us had always been quite conservative where money was concerned, and the realization that we were this way made us frequently wonder whether we ought to do things differently or, as they say, whether we ought to "get a little more fun out of life." This question seemed especially acute as we drove home that night. The immediate question was whether we should move to a nicer home, and the more I thought about it, about whether we could "afford" it, the more my economics training told me that the only way to really answer that question was to go through a process such as that outlined in this book. Consequently, we had a "retreat."

Feeling that the only way we could really take a good look at our situation was to get away for a few days, we left our children with my mother and went off together to a place where we could relax and forget the everyday press of events. Here we spent the better part of two days trying to forecast the amount of money we would need in order to enjoy the sort of future which we felt we would like to have.

Fortunately, it was not necessary for us to spend much time in stating our lifetime goal. This followed directly from our religion. We are members of a church that teaches that this life is a period in which we are each tested to determine our abililty to live together in peace and harmony under the direction of a wise and loving Father in Heaven. Our goal was thus to pass this test. In order to do this, we felt that we should follow the program which had been outlined by our church.

Our problem, then, was basically to estimate how much time and money would be required to live the program which we had already decided upon and how much would be available for other things such as a more elegant home. Consequently, we spent two days trying to predict such things as when we would need new cars, when we would need to replace our furnace, and when weddings would be coming along, and roughly how much each of these things would cost. What we were after, and all we could hope for anyway, were rough estimates, "ballpark" estimates if you prefer, for each of these expenses. At this first retreat we were not concerned with the time required to attain our goals, concentrating instead on the financial side of the question.

The result of our first retreat was a list. This list included, for all of the following categories, an estimate as to how much we would have to spend each year for the rest of our lives if we were to attain our goals in life. The categories were divided up into routine expenses on the one hand and nonroutine expenses on the other. The routine expenses were as follows:

- Automobile maintenance
- Automobile insurance
- Hobbies
- Haircuts
- Life Insurance
- House maintenance
- Taxes and insurance on house
- Weekend trips
- Furniture and appliance repair
- Food
- Rent
- Pest control
- Household goods insurance
- Job expenses
- Gasoline and oil
- Charitable contributions
- Professional dues and subscriptions
- Permanents and cosmetics
- Mortgages
- Utilities
- Annual family vacations
- Christmas
- Social obligations
- Entertainment
- Clothing
- Medical expenses
- Dental expenses
- Magazines and newspapers
- Tax preparation

The nonroutine expenses included the following:

- New cars
- Major trips
- Water heaters
- Living room sets
- Refrigerators
- Furnaces
- Bathroom remodeling
- Lessons for children
- Boat
- Ranges
- Weddings
- Cameras
- Stereos
- Visits to parents
- Dishwashers
- Garbage disposals
- Remodeling
- Legacy to our heirs
- Painting house
- Dining room sets
- Television sets
- Bedroom sets
- Carpeting and draperies
- Nursery school
- Braces on teeth
- Vacation home
- Freezers
- Education
- Second cars
- Projectors
- Washers and dryers
- Visits to children
- Funerals
- Vacuum cleaners
- New roofs

As you can see, we tried to make our list as comprehensive as we could. This is important, because anything which is left off the list reduces the value of the decision that is ultimately made. Many assumptions had to be made in compiling the list. For example, we had to estimate the number of children we would have, the rate of inflation which would prevail to the end of the period, the useful lives of each of our appliances, and so forth. The prices assumed for the various items on our list were ballpark figures as to what we might expect to pay for the type of item we had in mind and were based upon our own experience, a few phone calls, and a few department store catalogues.

Following our retreat, we did three things. First, I made an estimate as to the amount of after-tax income (whatever you do, **don't** forget about all of the various taxes you will be paying) we could expect to receive over the years from various sources. These sources included my job as a professor, any consulting I may be involved with, the expected return from some money we had available for investment, and the income I expected from my retirement program and from social security. Obviously, there were a lot of assumptions necessary here, but some idea was felt to be better than none. (Our stock of Type II assets was sufficiently small that we by-passed the step of estimating our income from this source alone and considered income from our Type I assets right from the start.) Second, we both tried to attach specific time requirements to the various things which would be necessary if we were to attain our goals. Some of these requirements were in the nature of what we thought would be required, and some were more in the nature of how much time we thought we would like to spend.

The items on our list of time requirements included the following:

Sleeping	Eating
Grooming	Relaxing
"Running around"	Prayer
Telephone	Daily chores
Exercising	Working
Self-improvement	Recreation
Scripture study	Church meetings
Other church responsibilities	Family nights
Routine shopping	Weekly chores
Time with children	Planning
Bill-paying	Socializing
Doctor visits	Sewing
Writing letters	Monthly chores
Vacations	Yearly chores
Illnesses	Dental visits

- Christmas shopping
- Haircuts and permanents
- Canning
- Remodeling
- Visits to relatives
- Planning Funerals
- Chores occurring less frequently than once a year
- Christmas cards
- Income tax preparation
- Retreats
- Shopping for major purchases
- Taking children to lessons
- Planning Weddings

Third, I prepared feasibility analyses for both time and money in the manner described above. We thus set the stage for our second retreat.

Our second retreat was somewhat like the first. We chose a nice cheerful place where we could relax and get free of everyday problems. Like the first, we made it a sort of working vacation. But it was also fundamentally different. At our first retreat we had been formulating our economic problem. At our second retreat we were solving it. Daydreaming and a pseudo-realism had prevailed before, but some truly hard decisions were required at the second.

The procedure itself was simple enough. It was exactly as outlined above. It consisted of adjusting and readjusting our feasibility worksheets until we had a solution which left no negative entries in Columns T4 and M5 and which we could not think of any way to improve upon. In doing this, a number of issues had to be faced. As the original motivation for the whole undertaking had been the question of a new house, we spent a considerable amount of time on this issue. The substitution of a larger stream of mortgage payments increased considerably the figures in Column M2, our money expenditures. How could we then make Column M5 nonnegative? We considered such options as removing certain items from our list of expenditures (a vacation home, a boat), dropping one of the retirement programs to which we had been contributing, reducing our insurance coverage, and the earning of extra income by either my wife or myself. Since, for us, Column T4 also had lots of negative figures, we had to consider which of our time expenditures to delete if we chose the extra income option. Essentially, we looked for options which might be available to us and then examined the implications of each for the figures on our worksheets. (We took a pocket calculator along with us, and you would be well-advised to do the same.) In doing so, we got a very clear understanding of the nature of the problem we were facing, we got a much clearer understanding of each other's needs and desires, and we came to grips with reality.

What ultimately emerged from our second retreat was, thus, a basic decision concerning nothing less than what we planned to do with the rest of our lives. (This decision was not actually made during the retreat itself, but came some time later after we had had time to digest the matters discussed at that time.) All that was then left was to write it all up neatly and prepare annual time and money budgets to give us direction over the following few years.

Was it worth all the trouble? Absolutely. I would recommend it to anyone.

For the first time in our lives we have really felt that we were in control of our lives, that we were making intelligent decisions, that we were actually doing the best that we could. For the first time in our lives we have been able to really communicate on money matters. This is, I suppose, because we both know the nature of the problem which we confront. We both know what the relevant issues are. We are also better able now to live our **own** lives. We are now making decisions on the basis of **our** goals and **our** expectations, these have all been made explicit, and if we decide to change them, we will be doing so for what we view as good and sufficient reasons. Furthermore, our children will also be more aware of the constraints under which we live when they become old enough for us to explain our solution to them. This, I feel, will make the division of household chores much more meaningful to them than it would otherwise have been, and will make us, as parents, **credible** when we say we cannot afford something. We will be able to show them in black and white exactly why we have made the decisions which we have, and we will understand each other better as a result. Finally, our decisions are now based on a more realistic view of our situation than was previously the case, they are more likely to produce the intended results, and we are **far** less likely to look back in 30 or 40 years and feel that we have wasted our lives. We have gotten our heads above the trees, so to speak, and have caught a glimpse of the forest. At least we think we have, and that is what really matters anyway.

Was it worth all the trouble? You'd better believe it.

Part II

How Value is Determined

In part I of this book, you were introduced to the concept of the lifetime budget and the process of constructing such a budget was explained. As a part of that process, it was necessary for you to make an estimate as to the amount of income you would have available during various future periods to satisfy the desires on your list. Making this estimate was an essential step in the process of allocation, but what you made was only an estimate. What your future income stream actually turns out to be will depend upon what you do with your assets. One part of this income stream will come from that part of your time which you devote to earning an income. The size of this portion will be influenced by your set of personal assets, especially by your set of skills and your psychological makeup. The other portion of your income stream will be influenced by your set of physical assets—your holdings of cash, real estate, common stocks, rare paintings, and the like. Either these assets or the services they provide can be sold and the proceeds used as income to satisfy your desires. You will thus want to apply that part of your time which is devoted to earning an income to that particular use where it will yield the largest income stream possible. Similarly, you will want to employ your physical assets in such a way that they will provide the largest possible fund for the satisfaction of your desires.

In order to accomplish these objectives, you must engage in a never-completed process of altering the content of your set of assets, removing assets whose value is low and acquiring assets whose value is higher. Thus, you must periodically decide which assets have the greatest value (that is, which assets will yield you the greatest stream of future satisfaction) and acquire them, disposing of whatever assets are necessary to accomplish this. You may, for example, exchange time and money for a certain skill which has greater value than the time and money needed to acquire it. Or you may exchange real estate for some shares of common stock having greater value than the real estate. Or you may exchange time, government bonds, and rare stamps for an improvement in your health. Whatever exchanges you actually make, the process of increasing your stream of present and future satisfaction is rather simple. You merely exchange your existing set of assets for a set which will yield a greater stream of satisfactions. So far, so good. But how can you identify those assets having the greatest value? How, indeed, can you determine the value of any asset at all, given that its value is merely a reflection of its ability to yield desire-satisfaction in the future and given that the future is uncertain? The simple answer is that you can't. And yet you must. Or rather you must try. You do, in fact, live in a world of uncertainty. You must, in fact, elect to hold one set of assets or another. And the only way to get the most out of life is to obtain that set of assets which has the greatest value of all those sets of assets which your current set of assets will enable you to obtain.

To help you do this is the task of Part II. It will not identify the valuable assets for you. Nothing can do that. It will, however, give you an understanding of the principles that determine the value of any asset. Armed with this understanding, you will be in a much better position to increase the value of your current asset holdings, or (what amounts to the same thing) to keep it from decreasing, than you would otherwise have been.

The Nature of Economic Life

In the following pages we will study the nature of economic life. This is essentially a study of the consequences of the independent actions of millions upon millions of people each trying to solve their own economic problems, that is, each trying to employ their assets so as to satisfy as many of their desires as possible. Our reason for studying this subject was stated above, namely, that only by doing so can you come to understand the forces which give value to an asset. And only by understanding such forces can you hope to adjust your own asset bundle so as to get the most out of life.

It should be clear from the very beginning that our study is concerned with the actions of human beings. All such actions result from the decisions of human beings. People act, institutions do not. People act, the environment does not. It is not a government that takes an action, not a corporation. It is a specific individual within a government or a corporation who acts. Such individuals will, to be sure, be greatly influenced by their positions within these institutions, but it is they who act, not the institutions themselves. The importance of such a seemingly obvious statement may not be apparent at first, but it will become more so as we proceed. With this then as an introduction, let us begin.

An economic system is basically a collection of people, of individual human beings. Each of these individuals is unique. Each has his or her own desires and his or her own set of assets with which to satisfy these desires. The actions of each of these individuals is motivated by one thing, the satisfaction of whatever desires they may have.

In saying that people are motivated by their desires, I do not mean to imply that they are all motivated by the desire to accumulate material wealth or power. Rather, I mean that each of us has certain things that we desire and that, given these desires, we try to satisfy them as best we can. We will not be concerned in this book with the desires themselves, only with the implications of our efforts to satisfy them. The desires themselves spring from many sources. Some of them come from the biological nature of our bodies. These would include desires such as those for warmth and for nourishment. Others result from our associations with other people. These are the desires for such things as clothing of a particular style, a house in a particular neighborhood, or a car of a particular make and year. Many of our desires result from the natural enviroment in which we find ourselves. Insects attack our gardens and must be combatted. Our water heaters fall victim to the process of rusting. We ourselves are under continual attack from unseen armies of bacteria, fungi, and viruses, all of which must be dealt with. Floods destroy our crops, winds destroy our homes, wood rots, termites attack our fence posts, and, finally, our bodies themselves wear out. All of these things generate desires on our part. Finally, we have desires such as those for adventure or for a sense of being loved, the source of which there is no point in even guessing at.

In addition to arising from a number of sources, our desires are continually changing. A new product appears on the market. We receive a new baby girl. We read a new book. Fads change. We simply grow older, and our children move away. Whatever the causes, our set of desires is not constant. It is dynamic. We don't know today what we will desire tomorrow.

Individuals thus have desires. They also have assets. As their desires are unique, so are their assets. One individual is tall, another is short. One can run fast. Another is born deaf and dumb. Each of us has his or her own set of assets, and included in this set are the following. First, we have our physical characteristics, that is, our degree of physical health, our physical beauty, our physical handicaps, how energetic we are, our muscular coordination, our ability to sing, to draw, to get by on six hours of sleep per day, our ability to do hard physical labor, and so forth. Next, we have our mental characteristics. These would include our ability to concentrate, our ability to carry through abstract reasoning, our ability to learn specific skills, our ability to remember. Third, each of us has accumulated a set of skills and pieces of information. Fourth, we each have a personality which is unique to us. Next, we each have a set of friends and associates that is uniquely ours. We also each occupy a specific place in the social order which gives us a certain degree of prestige, a certain influence upon other people. Another area in which we are unique is that of our imaginations, our ability to be creative and to see things from a new perspective. Each of us also possesses a specific way of looking at ourselves and at the world around us, a specific self-image, a specific philosophy of life, a specific religion.

In what follows, it will often be useful to refer to the set of assets noted thus far as constituting an individual's "human capital." In addition to our human capital, we also have physical possessions such as bank accounts, automobiles, houses, stocks and bonds, iron mines, oil wells, office buildings, factories, farms, stamp collections, silver coins, industrial machinery, and a host of others. Each of our collections of physical assets is, of course, unique.

Finally, in addition to our human capital and our physical assets, each of us has the time remaining between this moment and the end of our life.

Each individual is thus unique. He has a unique set of desires. He has a unique set of assets. But in one respect all individuals are alike. Each has an economic problem. Each possesses assets which are inadequate to enable him to satisfy all of his desires. Each must thus solve this economic problem. That is, each must use his or her assets in such a way as to satisfy his or her desires to the greatest possible degree, and it is the effort of each individual to do this which determines the nature of economic life.

The Division of Labor

Few, if any, of the desires of an individual are satisfied spontaneously by his environment. Indeed, those that are, such as the desire of our bodies for oxygen, are normally not thought of as desires at all. Rather, the satisfaction of our desires normally requires the conscious application of our assets.

In applying our assets to the satisfaction of our desires, each of us has a fundamental choice. We can either apply those assets to satisfy our needs directly (as we do when we brush the hair out of our eyes) or we can apply our assets in the context of the social division of labor.

What is the division of labor? It is the practice of individuals to "divide up" the tasks that they collectively desire accomplished. Some individuals grow the wheat, some individuals build the houses, some repair refrigerators, and some set broken bones. Each individual selects a specific service and specializes in the provision of that service. He then exchanges his service for the services of others. He thus satisfies his desires in a somewhat roundabout manner. He satisfies the desires of others, and they satisfy his desires in return.

Why would any individual choose to satisfy his desires indirectly through the division of labor when he could satisfy them directly? He does this because it is incomparably more efficient. That is to say, by entering into the division of labor he is able to satisfy his desires to a much greater degree than he ever could in isolation. Look around yourself. How many of the items which you take for granted each day would you have been able to provide all by yourself? Could you have built your refrigerator? What about your automobile or your television set? What about the paper from which this book is made or the ink with which it is printed? Now then, ask yourself this question. Could you have made them **all**? The answer is obvious. In the absence of the division of labor each of our lives would be something akin to an extended camping trip. Only this camping trip would be without the benefit of gas stoves, without nylon tents with aluminum poles, without steel camp saws, and perhaps even without matches. I believe it was Abraham Lincoln who stated that we are all ignorant depending upon the subject which is being considered. And this is certainly true. And yet how is it possible that such a collection of ignoramuses can enjoy wholesome diets, telephonic communication, air travel, thick carpets, and chocolate parfaits? It is because of the social division of labor, pure and simple. If we each had to learn how to produce all the things we enjoy, we would be living like cavemen. As a final endorsement of the division of labor, let me quote what is perhaps the most famous description of it that has ever been given. It is from the book **An Inquiry Into the Nature and Causes of the Wealth of Nations**, published in 1776 by Adam Smith, the virtual father of classical economics. According to Smith:

> "The greatest improvement in the productive powers of labour, and the greater part of the skill, dexterity, and judgment with which it is anywhere directed, or applied, seem to have been the effects of the division of labour.
>
> "The effects of the division of labour, in the general business of society, will be more easily understood, by considering in what manner it operates in some particular manufactures. It is commonly supposed to be carried furthest in some very trifling ones; not perhaps that it really is carried further in them than in others of more importance: but in those trifling manufactures which are destined to supply the small wants of but a small number of people, the whole number of workmen must necessarily be small; and those employed in every different branch of the work can

often be collected into that same workhouse, and placed at once under the view of the spectator. In those great manufactures, on the contrary, which are destined to supply the great wants of the great body of the people, every different branch of the work employs so great a number of workmen, that it is impossible to collect them all into the same workhouse. We can seldom see more, at one time, than those employed in one single branch. Though in such manufactures, therefore, the work may really be divided into a much greater number of parts, than in those of a more trifling nature, the division is not near so obvious, and has accordingly been much less observed.

"To take an example, therefore, from a very trifling manufacture; but one in which the division of labour has been very often taken notice of, the trade of the pin-maker; a workman not educated to this business (which the division of labour has rendered to a distinct trade), nor acquainted with the use of the machinery employed in it (to the invention of which the same division of labour has probably given occasion), could scarce, perhaps, with his utmost industry, make one pin a day, and certainly could not make twenty. But in the way in which this business is now carried on, not only the whole work is a peculiar trade, but it is divided into a number of branches, of which the greater part are likewise peculiar trades. One man draws out the wire, another straights it, a third cuts it, a fourth points it, a fifth grinds it at the top for receiving the head; to make the head requires two or three distinct operations; to put it on, is a peculiar business, to white the pins is another; it is even a trade by itself to put them into the paper; and the important business of making a pin is, in this manner, divided into about eighteen distinct operations, which, in some manufactories, are all performed by distinct hands, though in others the same man will sometimes perform two or three of them. I have seen a small manufactory of this kind where ten men only were employed, and where some of them consequently performed two or three distinct operations. But though they were very poor, and therefore but indifferently accommodated with the necessary machinery, they could, when they exerted themselves, make among them about twelve pounds of pins in a day. There are in a pound upwards of four thousand pins of a middling size. Those ten persons, therefore, could make among them up-

> wards of forty-eight thousand pins in a day. Each person, therefore, making a tenth part of forty-eight thousand pins, might be considered as making four thousand eight hundred pins in a day. But if they had all wrought separately and independently, and without any of them having been educated to this peculiar business, they certainly could not each of them have made twenty, perhaps not one pin a day; that is, certainly, not the two hundred and fortieth, perhaps not the four thousand eight hundredth part of what they are at present capable of performing, in consequence of a proper division and combination of their different operations."[1]

The division of labor does have some drawbacks. One is occasional unemployment. The hermit is never unemployed, but this does occur periodically with the division of labor. Another drawback of the division of labor is that it makes each of us dependent on other people for our very survival. There are very few really self-sufficient people on the earth today, and nearly all of them are members of the more primitive cultures. In the modern, industrialized countries (and in the developing countries as well) we are all interdependent. While the division of labor does, therefore, have some negative qualities, its incredible efficiency so far outweighs these drawbacks that it has been the universal form of economic organization throughout all of recorded history. Each individual selects one or a very few specialized areas of production and exchanges his output for the output of others.

The Search for a Specialty

Each individual thus finds it in his own best interest to satisfy the desires of others in order to satisfy his own desires. He does this because no one is likely to satisfy his desires without getting something in return. To quote Adam Smith again, "It is not from the benevolence of the butcher, the brewer, or the baker, that we expect our dinner, but from their regard to their own interest."[2] Each individual must,

---

[1]Adam Smith, **An Inquiry Into the Nature and Causes of the Wealth of Nations, Volume I,** (Printed for W. Strahan and T. Cadell, in the Strand, London, 1776), pp. 5-7.

[2]Ibid., p. 17.

therefore, decide how best to utilize his assets in satisfying the needs of other people. The process of doing so constitutes his search for a specialty.

The search for a specialty is carried on in the context of uncertainty. The desires of other individuals are not known, their future desires are unknown even to themselves, and the individual in question is not even aware of all the services which he may be capable of providing. How then does he choose a specialty?

There exists at any given time a set of services which the individual knows that he is capable of providing. These "services" should be understood to include not only the provision of his time, his skills, and his knowledge, but the provision of the services of any of his other assets (such as his land or his money) as well. The act of providing each of these services itself yields the individual some degree of satisfaction or dissatisfaction, that is, he enjoys providing some of them (such as driving a tour bus) and dislikes providing others (such as washing dishes). Given his unique set of assets, each of these services can be provided by him at some specific rate. Finally, each of the services would, if performed, satisfy the desires of other people to a given degree. These other people would thus be willing to exchange a certain portion of their own assets for the service, and this amount is indicated by the current price which the service commands. Thus, by providing any given service, the individual can expect to receive a given set of rewards. This set will consist of the monetary return he expects to receive in the form of payment and the nonmonetary rewards he expects to get from the act of performing the service itself. This expected set of rewards from providing any given service is only that, however, an **expected** set of rewards. It is not guaranteed. People may well change their minds about the value which the service has to them. If this happens, the monetary part of the reward will change. Alternatively, the individual himself may change his attitude toward the act of providing it once he learns more about it. Thus, the rewards to be expected from the provision of any given service are uncertain. Furthermore, the individual is not even aware of all the specialties from which he might select.

How then is the decision made? It is made somewhat as follows. The individual simply begins seeking alternatives and investigating them one by one. In each case he determines, as best he can, the degree to which his particular set of assets would enable him to provide the service in question, the degree to which he would enjoy the act of providing it, and the degree to which his provision of it would satisfy the desires of other people. He then estimates the return to **him** from providing the service, that is, the monetary and nonmonetary rewards he can expect from providing the quantity and quality of the service which he can expect to provide. This examination of alternatives will continue until finally, in the mind of the individual, the likelihood of finding an alternative preferable to the most attractive of those of which he is already aware is not sufficiently high to justify further search. At that point, he decides to provide that service which offers him the greatest expected reward of all those of which he is aware. The greater the stock of assets that an individual possesses, the longer he will be able to continue his search. This is because the search process itself is expensive in that if he were not searching, he could be receiving the rewards from providing a service. The better able he is to forego those rewards, that is, the better able he is to provide for his current needs from his own assets, the longer he will be able to continue the search. And the longer he continues the search, the more desirable the outcome is likely to be.

The Entrepreneur

For each of the specialized services which an individual might choose to provide, there exists a specific stream of expected rewards stretching into the future. Some of these reward streams, such as that for being a government employee, are relatively predictable. Others, such as the reward stream for opening a hardware store, are less so. In the latter case, there exists a great deal of uncertainty about the size of the reward stream, and anyone who undertakes to provide that service runs a very considerable risk that the stream will turn out to be very low or even negative.

Certain individuals are more willing to bear such risk than others. Although the reasons for this ability or willingness to bear risk are not fully known, one major reason has to do with the set of assets an individual possesses. The risk inherent in providing any service is the risk that it may yield a reward which is low or even negative. It is the ability of an individual to survive such an unfavorable outcome and go on with his life which determines his willingness to take the chance, and this ability is directly tied to his set of assets. A person with large holdings of physical assets or with a great deal of "human capital" (a good set of skills, for example, or a large set of influential friends) is much more willing to undertake a risk of a given magnitude than is one with fewer physical assets or less human capital. The loss of $50,000 would be unpleasant for some people, but it would be an absolute disaster for others. For some it would mean a smaller legacy for their heirs, for others it would mean a life of poverty.

There thus exists a group of people, those whose asset stocks are relatively large, who are, on the one hand, more able than others to conduct lengthy searches for opportunities, and, on the other hand, more willing than others to bear the risk of an unfavorable outcome. From this group come what are frequently called the **entrepreneurs**, a set of people who play an exceedingly important role in the economic process.

There are two types of entrepreneurs: speculators and innovators. A speculator is an individual who acquires an asset, such as a piece of land, which he believes will increase in value and then holds it for a period of time hoping that this indeed will be the case. He does nothing whatever to the asset itself. He merely owns it. If it does increase in value, he sells it and receives the increase in value as a speculative profit. If it decreases in value, he receives a speculative loss. His role in the economic process is that of bearing risk.

The innovator, on the other hand, plays a much more active role than does the speculator. What he does is, first, discover opportunities where existing assets can be combined **in new ways** such that they will produce something of greater value than they yielded before. Thus, the innovator seeks ways in which assets such as skills, land, time, and money can be used to make new products and ways in which old products can be made using new production processes. Once he has discovered such an opportunity, the second part of his role is to bear the risk inherent in putting his innovation into practice. For example, assume that an innovator believes that a particular town would be a good place in which to establish a laundromat. On the basis of this belief, he rents a building, he hires other individuals to remodel it and to install the necessary equipment, he borrows money to purchase the washing machines, and he oversees the work as it proceeds. When all is in readiness, he opens up for business. Whether or not he gets a single customer, he is legally obligated to pay the workers, to pay interest on and repay the loan, and to pay the rent on the building. He thus bears the risk that he was wrong and that the value of the laundromat to the economy is not greater than that of the labor, the capital,[3] and the building which were required to create it. If this turns out to be the case, then it is he to whom the creditors will turn, and it is he who will be taken to court if he cannot pay his debts. He can turn to no one. No one has signed a contract to patronize his laundromat. His obligations are legal obligations to pay fixed sums of money. His potential receipts

[3]Capital is defined in detail on page 45. For the present, just think of it as what is produced in the economy in excess of what is consumed.

are whatever they turn out to be. This is the nature of the risk that he bears. And what is his reward for providing this risky service? If the income of the laundromat exceeds the expenses required to operate it, he receives the difference as profit. In this case, he has literally **created value** through his innovation, and the value created goes to him as profit. If the expenses of the laundromat exceed its income, then he has literally **destroyed value**, and he is the individual whose assets are reduced.

It may be worth pausing for a moment to consider again what has happened here. Initially, there were some workers, there was a building, and there was some capital. Each of these "factors of production" (defined roughly in what follows as inputs into the productive process) had a particular market value. The labor was worth a certain wage, the building was worth a certain rental, and the use of the capital was worth a certain amount of interest. These values, which were the prices the innovator paid for them, reflected the values of what they would have been used to produce if it were not for the project of the innovator. That is to say, these prices reflected the "opportunity cost" to society of using them on the innovator's project rather than in their best alternative use. If the product that they produce for the innovator, in this case the service which the laundromat provides, proves to be worth more than the inputs cost, then the new product is worth more to society than what society was forced to do without in order to enjoy the presence of the laundromat. There is now more value than there was before, people's desires are now being satisfied to a greater degree than was previously the case, and the increase in this satisfaction is the direct result of the service of the innovator in combining the inputs in a new way and bearing the risk inherent in doing this. This is the source of innovative profit, the income of the innovator-entrepreneur.

The Worker, the Capitalist, and the Landowner

So much for the entrepreneurs. We have seen their role in the economic process and the nature of their incomes. What about the other individuals who provide productive services? How do their incomes arise, and how do their roles differ from that of the entrepreneurs? The individuals with whom we are now concerned are those who provide the various labor skills required to produce anything, those who furnish the raw materials necessary to the productive process, and those who furnish the capital necessary for innovation to take place at all. For convenience, we will refer to these individuals as workers, landowners, and capitalists, respectively.

The essential difference between the incomes which accrue to the worker, the landowner, and the capitalist and the income which accrues to the entrepreneur is that the former is relatively certain while the latter is not. A worker, for example, sells his services in much the same way that an entrepreneur sells his product. The essential difference is that the worker, the landowner, and the capitalist provide their services only after they have found a buyer and have agreed upon a price. An entrepreneur, on the other hand, provides his services without any such assurance. In the example noted earlier, the innovator put together the laundromat with no guarantee at all as to the number of customers he might expect. The workers who worked for him, however, received legally-enforceable claims for wages before they provided any service at all. So did the landlord and the money-lender. The incomes of the worker, the landlord, and the capitalist are not certain, of course. They are only relatively certain. Their claims are legally enforceable, but it could well be the case that the innovator will be unable to pay his debts. In this case, they will be forced to settle for less than the full amount of their claims. Their incomes are more certain than that of the entrepreneur, however, who has no legally-enforceable claim whatsoever.

The roles of the worker, the landowner, and the capitalist also differ significantly from that of the innovator. His role is to find opportunity and to bear risk. Theirs are to carry out the instructions of the innovator. Since he is paying for their services, these services are under his control. Since no one is obliged to pay the entrepreneur, he is under no obligation to carry out the instructions of anyone. The innovator has freedom of action but no security. The landlord, the worker, and the capitalist have contractual security but are also bound by contractual obligations. Of course, as we saw earlier, it was at least partly the underlying security inherent in the entrepreneur's superior assets which made him an entrepreneur in the first place. Thus, while he lacks security with respect to any given undertaking, he likely has a good deal of security when his situation is considered as a whole. At least it likely appears to him that he does.

Markets, Exchange, and Value

At the beginning of Part II, it was stated that in order to get the most that you can out of life it was essential that you continually seek to alter your stock of assets so as to always hold that set having the greatest possible value. This was the set which would enable you to satisfy more of your desires than any other set which you might be able to hold. It was also stated that it was the objective of Part II to explain the forces which determine asset values, thus increasing your chances of selecting assets the values of which would increase. It is to that task which we now turn.

Thus far, we have seen that an economy consists of individuals, each having specific desires and a specific set of assets. We saw that, in order to get a maximum of desire-satisfaction from his assets, each individual was compelled to enter into the social division of labor, satisfying the desires of others in order that they, in turn, might satisfy his desires. We then described the process by which each individual enters into the division of labor, that is, how he selects a specialty. Finally, we noted that certain individuals play the role of entrepreneurs. To understand the forces which determine value, we must look at what happens next. The process is as follows.

An innovative entrepreneur, in the course of his search for a specialty, comes upon an opportunity which he feels is sufficiently attractive to justify exploiting. This opportunity consists of a new way in which existing factors of production (that is, existing labor skills, capital, and natural resources) can be combined, a way which the innovator believes will yield an output having greater value than the factors of production which went into it. It is this increase in value which he hopes to capture as profit. Having made his decision to innovate, the innovator next selects a productive process. It may be possible for him to produce his new product in a variety of ways. That is to say, he may really have come upon a set of many possible innovations from which he may choose. He might, for example, select a production process using simple tools and highly-skilled workers. On the other hand, he may select a process using semi-skilled workers and a much more complex set of machinery. He might decide to produce his product out of plastic, out of steel, or out of aluminum. He may decide to produce it in one location rather than another. He must decide about the informational aspects of his new product. That is, he must decide how to inform people that it exists, how best to describe the benefits which it offers them, and how best to tell them what it will cost. At any rate, he must select a productive process. Once he selects that process which he expects to be the most efficient, that is, to achieve his chosen end at the smallest overall cost, he must select a level of output. He does this by estimating the quantity of the product which he can sell at various prices and the cost of producing these various quantities and then selecting that quantity at which the expected profit (that is, the expected sales revenue minus the expected cost of production) will be the greatest. This choice determines the size of the production facilities which he will utilize (that is, his "factory"), the rate at which he will utilize those facilities, and the price which he will charge for the product. Having made all these decisions, he next obtains the necessary productive factors. He hires a set of workers having the proper set of skills and knowledge, he obtains the necessary tools, raw materials, and production site, and he borrows the capital with which to finance the project. In doing this, he undertakes contractual obligations to pay the wages, interest, and rent necessary to obtain these factors.

Having obtained the necessary factors of production, he next organizes them and directs their efforts so as to produce the product he has in mind. If all goes well, that is, if the production process he has selected actually produces the product desired, he offers his product for sale. It should be clearly understood that the product which he produces is more than merely a physical item or service. It includes, of course, the physical item or service, but it also includes information. Along with the physical item or service itself, the innovator must produce information. He must inform potential buyers that his product exists, he must tell them how it can satisfy their desires, and he must let them know how much it will cost them to enjoy it. A consideration of the information that accompanies a physical product or service is absolutely essential in understanding the output of the innovator. Thus, when we say that he offers his product for sale, we mean that he accompanies this offer with some type of promotional effort designed to inform potential buyers of the three things noted earlier, namely, that the product exists, what it will do for them, and what it will cost.

Once the product of the innovator is offered for sale, all individuals, as consumers, must respond. As was noted earlier, each individual has an economic problem of his very own. Each of them must solve this problem as best he can, and, as we saw in Part I, the way to solve this problem is to draw up a budget. Thus, each individual has a budget. Each individual does not have a budget in the sense that you have a budget, that is, in the sense that you have a budget if you have followed the instructions given in Part I. That is to say, each individual does not have a budget that is written out and reflects a serious consideration of his true desires and capabilities. But he has a budget nonetheless. Indeed, it could hardly be otherwise. Each penny of his income goes **somewhere.** Each second of his time is spent at **something.** All of his physical assets are held in **some** form. And the decisions as to how to spend his income, how to spend his time, and the form in which to hold his physical assets were made by him. Merely because they may not have been made in a logical, well-thought-out manner does not mean that they do not constitute his budget. Together, they specify exactly how he chooses to allocate his time, income, and capital so as to satisfy his desires to the greatest degree possible. They thus make up his budget.

Each individual responds to the new product of the entrepreneur by, in effect, revising his budget. He now has new knowledge which was absent when his inital budget was drawn up. He now knows (or does not know) of the existence of a new product which is alleged to be able to help him in certain ways and which will, if purchased, cost him a certain amount of money. He must thus answer the following question. How shall I alter my budget in light of this new information? In other words, he must decide how much of the new product to purchase and, if he decides to purchase any, which other items to sacrifice in order to make available the funds necessary to do this.

After this revision of his budget is complete, each individual can be said to "demand" a certain number of units of the new product. This demand is the number of units of that product which he elects to include in his revised budget. He has a demand, in this sense, for each of the products or services in existence. If each individual demands a certain quantity of the new product, then, taken together, all individuals as a group demand a quantity of the product which is the sum of the quantities demanded by the various individuals separately. This is the quantity which the innovator will sell at the price he is charging, and the joint determination of this amount by consumers constitutes their response to the innovation.

Thus, the entrepreneur innovates and the consumers respond. As they respond, they provide information. Whereas initially, the entrepreneur was basing his innovative activity on what he **thought** the response of consumers would be, he now **knows** what their response was like. Thus, he has more information on which to base his next move. Similarly, he has more information on the costs of producing his product. He has now actually produced some of it. He knows the problems involved. He knows whether or not his initial estimates as to input requirements were accurate. He has gained **experience**.

Based upon this experience, this new information, the entrepreneur will alter his behavior. He now has a more accurate expectation as to how much of the product can be sold at various prices. He now has a better idea as to what it will actually cost him to produce the product. Based upon this new information, he will revise his decision concerning the level of output and the price to be charged. He may also revise his decision as to which productive process to employ and what productive facilities to utilize (but this is less likely since he must live within his existing facilities to a certain degree). He may well alter the information which he is disseminating about the product.

Thus, during the next period, the entrepreneur will innovate again. He may offer the product at a somewhat different price. He may alter the nature of the product itself. He may produce at a new level of production, possibly using a new productive process. At any rate, the consumers will respond to his new innovation. That is to say, they will once again redraw their budgets. In doing so, they too will be basing their actions on new information. To begin with, the innovator will now be supplying new information as to the price and characteristics of the product. In addition, the consumers will also have gained experience. Many of them will have tried the product. They will **know** how well it satisfies their desires. They will tell others about their experience, and these others will take these opinions into consideration. Based upon this new information, each consumer will once again decide how much he or she will demand of the product, and the sum of these decisions constitutes the response of the consumers to the revised action of the entrepreneur.

This then is the essence of the market process. An entrepreneur innovates and offers his output to consumers. The consumers each respond by revising their budget allocations. The result is an increase in the information available to both sides. Based on this new information, the entrepreneur innovates again. Based on their experience and the new offer, the consumers again revise their purchasing behavior. The result of these actions by both buyers and sellers is that even more information is obtained. The view of the entrepreneur as to the demand for his product and the cost of producing it improves again. The view of consumers as to the qualities of the product improves. And both again revise their actions, the entrepreneur seeking that combination of product characteristics, information, quantity of output, price, and productive process which will yield him the greatest possible profit, and the consumer seeking that budget allocation which will yield him a maximum of desire satisfaction. By this process of venture and response, each of the actors in the drama feels his or her way through the mists of uncertainty in pursuit of their view of their own self-interest. This is the basic process upon which an understanding of the determinants of value must be built.

The Economic Pie: What Flavor It is, How It is Baked, and How It Is Divided Up

Have you ever wondered why resources are used as they are? When you think about it, the resources which constitute the earth and the skills possessed by its people could be used in a very large number of ways. And yet, when you look around you realize that they are being used in very specific ways. Only certain items are being produced. Production is, in each instance, being carried on in one specific way. And each product is being consumed by a specific set of individuals. What determines this? What determines, in other words, the answers to the following three questions? Which items are produced? How are they produced? Who consumes them?

Consider the first question, "Which items are produced?" At any given time, there exist a large number of consumers and a large number of innovative entrepreneurs. Each entrepreneur is engaged in the process of innovating and offering the resulting product for sale. Each consumer is engaged in the process of revising his budget in accordance with the changing set of products and services which is available. The consumers are passing judgement, so to speak, on the innovations of the entrepreneurs. Certain of these judgements will be favorable, and certain will be unfavorable.

If the consumers' judgement of an innovation is favorable, then the entrepreneur responsible for it will be rewarded. Since consumers do, in fact, place a higher value on the output than was originally placed on the set of inputs needed to produce it, a surplus is available which accrues to the entrepreneur as profit. Products which yield profits are produced again.

If the consumers' judgement of an innovation is unfavorable, then the entrepreneur involved will find that there is simply no positive level of output which he can select which will yield him a profit. That is to say, there is simply no positive level of output for which consumers will pay more for the product than must be paid in order to obtain the productive factors needed to produce it. Products such as these are not produced again.

Thus, at any given time, the products being produced are those which entrepreneurs believe will be judged favorably by consumers, thereby yielding them a profit. This set of products will change over time. Each new innovation that takes place will alter the budget allocation of each consumer. It will thus alter the demand of each consumer **for each and every product**. Thus, the producers of some products which have been profitable find that they are no longer so. The producers of other products find that the new innovations have made them even more profitable than before. The continuing flow of innovations has a different impact on each existing product. The profitability of any given product will be altered by each new innovation that occurs. Some innovations will have a greater impact than others, of course, but each of them will have an impact. The implication of this fact is that it is never possible for an entrepreneur to rest on the results of past innovation. He must treat the decisions of each new producing period as constituting a brand new innovation. This is because they do. Cost conditions are not the same. Demand conditions have changed as well.

Uncertainty, while it may be considerably reduced by experience, never entirely disappears.

While it is not clear in advance just how each new innovation is going to affect the profitability of any given existing product, one tendency is clear. That is that those products which have been especially profitable in the past will likely be adversely affected by the new innovations. The reason for this is quite simple. Once an entrepreneur has made a successful innovation, he has revealed new information to other prospective innovators. He has shown them that there exists a strong demand on the part of consumers for a certain type of product, namely, the one he has produced. If a strong demand exists for one product, it will then be reasoned, perhaps a similar demand exists for a second product only slightly different from the first. Hence, there will be a tendency for subsequent innovation to take the form of imitating the successful innovation. Inasmuch as any new product will tend to draw customers primarily from products similar to itself, the imitative innovations will very likely reduce the profitability of the imitated.

You should note, however, that this tendency does not work in reverse. An innovation which has produced unusually low profits in the past will not be moved into a more profitable situation by subsequent innovation. It is possible, of course, that this will happen, but it is by no means certain. What is crucial is the reason for the poor profit performance. If it is due to a deficiency of demand, then the situation may well improve with time as innovation elsewhere increases the wealth of the economy as a whole and thus the demand for all products (including the one under consideration) and as the producers of close substitutes become discouraged and cease production. If, on the other hand, the poor profit performance is due to an inefficient productive process, there is probably nothing that can save the situation.

The products being produced at any given time are, thus, those which entrepreneurs expect to yield a profit. Let us now consider the question of how these products are produced. This question can be answered very quickly once it is recalled that each innovation consists not only of selecting a product but of selecting a method of producing it as well. Thus, in passing judgement on each innovation, consumers are also passing judgement upon methods of production. Inasmuch as a low-cost method of production allows an innovator to offer his product to the consumer at a lower price, consumers tend to view innovations employing such methods much more favorably than those employing high-cost methods of production. Thus, the set of products being produced at any given moment will be produced using relatively low-cost methods of production, and lower-cost methods will replace higher-cost methods as time goes on. Producers employing high-cost methods will simply be unable to sell their products for enough to yield them a profit.

Turning now to our third question, let us see what determines the pattern of consumption, why certain individuals consume much and other individuals consume little. At first glance, the answer to this question seems obvious. Each individual has a budget indicating what he will consume, and the size of each individual's budget depends upon his income. Thus, those individuals who have high incomes consume a lot, and those with low incomes only consume a little.

But what determines income? This is the real question.

The income of each individual is produced by his performing a service for other people. Essentially, he must place at their disposal either his human capital, his nonhuman capital, or his natural resources. For this service, he receives an income in the form of rent, wages, interest, or profit. The specific amount of income in each case depends upon two things, the amount of the service he provides and the amount which others are willing to pay for the service. Thus, the income an individual derives from his capital is determined by how much capital he loans out and the interest rate he receives. His income from natural resources depends upon how much of them are rented or sold and the rental or sales price per unit of each, his income from labor depends upon the number of hours worked and the wage rate, and his income from entrepreneurial activity depends upon how successful his innovation or speculation turns out to be.

Now the quantity of these assets that any given individual possesses (his human capital, his nonhuman capital, his stock of natural resources, and his time) is determined by a variety of things. Some of it is the result of past economic activity. A profitable entrepreneurial venture, for example, will increase one's set of assets in the following period. A second part is determined by inheritance. Some people are born healthy, and others are not. Some are born to wealthy families, and others are born to no families at all. Finally, a third part of each individual's asset stock is determined by what is commonly known as luck. One person wins a million dollars in a lottery, and another loses both legs in an auto accident. Suffice it to say that an individual's assets are determined by a variety of things. Fortunately, the matter of how the asset holdings of individuals come to be is not our major concern here. We are concerned with what determines their value. We are interested, in other words, with what it is that determines the wage rate for a particular skill, the interest rate for a loan of a particular duration, and the rent for a particular piece of land. We have already considered those factors which determine the profitability of a given innovation.

Let us first consider the case of labor. What is it that determines the wage rate for a specific labor skill such as typing? Basically, the wage is determined through the interaction of two groups of people—those who might supply this skill and those who might hire typists.

Each individual, as we have said so many times before, has a budget. This budget specifies, among other things, the amount of time that that individual will spend supplying each and every skill that there is. One of these skills is that of typing. Thus, each individual, writing up his budget in the context of the set of prices which he faces, specifies the number of hours which he plans to spend working as a typist. By adding these figures up over all individuals, we obtain the number of hours which individuals as a group plan to spend as typists in the coming period.

Each innovator is also engaged in planning his activities for the period under discussion. During this period, he plans to produce a specific product in a specific quantity using a specific productive process at a specific place. Now the decision to produce a specific product with a specific process at a specific volume implies a decision to hire a specific quantity of each productive factor. These quantities will be required to meet the production plan. Thus, each entrepreneur in deciding what to produce, how to produce it, and how much of it to produce is at the same time deciding to hire a specific quantity of hours of typing skill. By summing these quantities over all entrepreneurs, we determine the number of hours of typing skill which entrepreneurs as a group are planning to hire.

There thus exist two sets of plans, those plans of individuals to spend a certain number of hours being typists and those plans of entrepreneurs to hire a certain number of hours of typing skill. Either the number of hours in the former will exceed that in the latter, the number of hours in the latter will exceed that in the former, or the two will be equal. Take the first instance, the case in which more typing skill is offered than is desired. In this case, something like the following will occur. Both the prospective typists and the prospective employers, being unaware of the others' identities, must seek each other out. They will thus begin a search. Each typist will be seeking that employer willing to pay the highest wage, and each employer will be seeking the typist who is willing to work for the lowest wage. Inasmuch as search activity is bothersome and time consuming, the searches will not continue indefinitely. Rather, hirings will take place whenever the potential typists and the potential employers involved feel it is not worth continuing the search further. So long as either the job-seeker or the potential employer feel that it is worth looking further, they will do so rather than signing a contract. In this way, typists and employers are brought together. Those typists who are very much in need of income will take jobs sooner at lower wages. Those employers who are very much in need of typists will sign contracts earlier at higher wages. Those typists and those employers better able to sustain a search effort will sign contracts later on at wages determined by the state of the market. Since we are considering the case in which the number of typists available exceeds the number of typists desired in the prevailing wage range, the prospective typists will be at a disadvantage in the bargaining process. The prospective employers will be less anxious to sign contracts than will they. This is because there will always be another typist for the would-be employer to interview should the present applicant refuse to sign, but there will not always be another employer for the prospective typist to interview should the negotiations fail. Thus, the potential typists will be more willing to make concessions than will the employers, and the wage rate at which succeeding contracts are signed will drift lower. It could even fall below the wage at which the more anxious job-seekers were hired earlier. It should be remembered that there is no reason to expect all equally-efficient typists to earn equal wages. This would only occur if all typists and all employers had perfect knowledge of what each typist was earning. Then those typists earning low wages would approach those employers paying high wages and offer to work for less than the employers are then paying or those employers paying high wages would fire the high-priced typists and approach the low-priced typists with offers of wages higher than they had been receiving but lower than they had been paying. By this process, the wages of all typists of equal skill would move toward equality. In the absence of perfect information, wage differences will persist, being smaller, of course, to the degree that information is available.

The wage level will not drift down without limit, however. As the level of wages falls, certain job-seekers will cease to seek jobs as typists. As you recall, the number of hours any individual plans to work at any occupation is determined in the context of his overall budgeting decision. As the wage rate for typists declines relative to that for other occupations, certain individuals will find it in their interest to revise their budgets in such a way that they allocate less of their time to supplying typing skills. Thus, the number of hours of typing skill offered by all individuals combined will decline. Similarly, as the wage rate for typists declines, employers will find that those production processes which require relatively more hours of typing skill will decline in cost relative to those processes which require fewer hours. Thus, certain entrepreneurs will find it in their interest to alter their plans and produce their products with processes which require more typists. As they do so, the number of hours of typing skill sought by employers as a group will increase. As the number of hours of typing skill offered by job-seekers falls relative to the number sought by potential employers, a shift will take place in the relative bargaining power of the two sets of parties. No longer will typists be quite so fearful of failing to sign a contract. No longer will employers be quite so confident that another typist will be along if the present one gets away. Thus, the prospective typists will become less and less willing to accept jobs with wages lower than those generally prevailing, and employers will become less and less likely to request that they do so. At some point, as the number of job-seekers declines and the number of potential hirers increases, the relative bargaining power of these two groups will become approximately equal, and when that occurs the wage rate will cease falling and will stabilize. The wage rate works as a sort of signal. When it is rising, it signals to individuals that it is in their interest to revise their budgets in favor of typing and to entrepreneurs that it is in their interest to produce with processes requiring fewer typists. When it is falling, the signals sent to entrepreneurs and to prospective typists are reversed. Only when the responses to the signal are such as to bring the number of typing hours offered into rough equality with the number of hours sought will the wage rate stabilize.

Movements in the wage rate for typists are thus determined by the relationship between the number of hours offered for sale by typists and the number of hours desired by prospective employers. What are the things that affect these two numbers? Recall again that the number of hours which each individual plans to spend providing typing skills is determined in the context of his entire budgeting decision. This means that it is affected by a very large number of things. Most obvious may be the wage rate offered in other occupations. If the wage for stenographers, for example, increases, then certain individuals will find that they can satisfy more of their desires by revising their budgets, supplying fewer hours of typing skill and more hours of stenographic skill. This will affect the number of hours offered by all typists combined and will tend to raise the wage rate for typists. Another determinant of the wage rate for typists is the information possessed by actors in the economic drama. Suppose it were discovered that typing is a major cause of arthritis. Given this new piece of information, each individual would revise his budget, presumably in the direction of offering fewer hours of typing skill. This would reduce the aggregate number of hours offered, it would increase the relative bargaining power of the job-seekers, and it would raise the wage rate. Alternatively suppose that a new production process was discovered which required fewer typists than the previously existing processes. If this process was lower-cost than the previous processes, then certain entrepreneurs would find it in their interest to adopt it, and the number of hours of typing skill sought by entrepreneurs would decline. This would shift the relative bargaining power in favor of employers and would cause a decline in the wage level for typists.

The wage level for typists will also be affected by other things. Suppose for example, that a new product is developed. The existence of the new product will lead each individual to revise his existing budget. Those who elect to purchase some of the new product must find the money to do this by making revisions somewhere else. Thus, the appearance of the new product will lead to a fall in the demand for various other products and services. Now the least-cost process for the production of the new product and the least-cost process for that of each of the other products affected will require a certain number of hours of typing skill. As the relative outputs of the various products are adjusted by entrepreneurs to reflect the revised pattern of demands, the number of typists needed for the production of certain products will decline and the number needed for the production of certain others will increase. If the number of new typists sought for the expanding industries exceeds the number of typists laid off by those industries whose outputs are declining, then the total number of typists sought will increase, relative bargaining power will shift in favor of the jobseekers, and the wage rate will rise. If the number of new typists sought is less than the number laid off, the reverse will be true.

As a final determinant of the wages of typists, let us look at changes in the levels of wealth of the individuals in the economy. An increase in an individual's wealth will lead him to revise his budgetary allocations. This can affect the wage of typists in a number of ways. First of all, there is an impact on the number of hours of typing skill demanded. This is due to the alterations in the pattern of consumption desired by the individual whose wealth has increased. This individual will elect to buy more of some items, such as summer homes and maid service, and less of others, such as day-old bread and low-priced clothing. As noted earlier, the least-cost production process for each product requires a certain number of typing hours per unit of output of the product. Thus, the effect on the total demand for typing skills depends upon the relative change in the demands for those products using many typists and those using fewer typists as the wealth of consumers expands.

There is also an impact on the number of hours of typing skill offered at any given wage rate. As an individual's wealth increases, he feels the need for additional income less urgently. Money becomes less of a limitation on his ability to satisfy his desires, and the lack of time becomes more of a problem for him than the lack of money. As this occurs, he will revise his budget allocations—he will begin buying time with money. He will, in other words, spend less time working. He will hire other individuals to do jobs which he previously did for himself, and he will spend less time working for others. If one of the jobs which he elects to spend less time at is typing, then the total number of hours of typing skill offered for sale will decline. In this way, changes in the wealth of the individuals in an economy will affect the level of wages in any occupation, including that of typists.

Having considered those things which determine the value of labor, let us now turn to the value of a natural resource such as land. What determines the value of a given piece of land?

Returning again to fundamentals, recall that each individual must make a budgetary decision. As part of that decision he must decide how to employ each of his assets in order to satisfy as many of his desires as possible. In doing so, he will decide what to do with each piece of land he controls. Some of this land may be devoted to personal use, such as pasture for a riding horse. Some will be placed at the disposal of others so as to produce income. Thus, in the act of solving its own economic problem, each household offers certain pieces of land to others, either for sale or for rent. The set of all individuals will thus offer a set of pieces of land to potential renters or purchasers.

Now each of these pieces of land is unique. Each has its own set of characteristics such as fertility, slope, location, access to water, and the like. Therefore, each piece of land will attract a unique set of potential land-users. Some of these potential land-users will be individuals desiring the land for consumption purposes. They may, for example, want it for a summer cottage. Others will desire to use the land as an input into an entrepreneurial venture, such as the growing of crops. Whatever the use to which a given potential land-user desires to put the land, however, each must decide the maximum amount that he is willing to pay for the use of the land rather than doing without it. For those desiring the land for consumption, this means answering the question, "How much am I willing to sacrifice in other areas in order to enjoy the use of this particular piece of land?" For those desiring to use the land as a productive factor, this means answering the question, "How much can I pay for the use of this piece of land before it would be cheaper for me to produce my product using a productive process which does not require it?" In answering these questions, each potential land-user thus arrives at the maximum amount which he would be willing to pay for the use of the piece of land in question. We will refer to this maximum amount as his "reservation price" for the use of the land.

Now then, how is the value of the land established? Basically, the landowner and the various potential land-users seek each other out, and an agreement is reached. Either the landowner will let it be known that the land is available or else the potential land-users will approach the landowner and offer to pay him for its use. Whichever sequence occurs, the potential land-users will approach the landowner one-by-one and make their offers to him. The size of these offers will be either the reservation prices of the particular persons making them or something lower if they believe they can obtain its use for less. Since the more offers the landowner receives the higher the highest of these offers is likely to be, it is in the landowner's interest to notify as many people as possible that he is interested in receiving offers for the use of the land. Thus, he will devote assets to publicizing this fact. As each successive offer is made, the landowner must decide whether to accept or reject it. He will decide to accept an offer when, in his opinion, it appears that the likelihood of receiving an offer preferable to the best one already received is not sufficiently high to justify further negotiation and when the offer exceeds his own reservation price for the use of the land. At this point, a contract will be signed and the value of the use of the land will have been determined.

Will the land be rented or sold? The answer depends upon the relative views of the landowner and the potential land-user having the highest reservation price as to the future value of the use of the land. Inasmuch as the value of the land to any individual (that is, his reservation price) is that amount which he would be willing to pay for the right to receive the future stream of monetary and nonmonetary benefits which the land will produce, the value of the land to him will be higher the larger he perceives this stream to be. Thus, if the landowner views this stream as smaller than the potential land-user, his reservation price will be less than the offer he recieves and the land will be sold. If, on the other hand, the landowner views this stream as greater than other people view it, his reservation price for the land will be greater than theirs. In this case he will find no one willing to pay him what he thinks the land is worth, and he will not sell the land. It does not follow, however, that he will then use the land himself. There may well exist an individual whose reservation price for the right to use the land over **all** future periods is less than the landowner's but whose reservation price for the right to use the land for a **limited number** of future periods is greater. If so, this individual will offer the owner an amount for this more limited use of the land which exceeds the owner's reservation price, and an agreement will be signed wherein the owner agrees to "rent out" the land (that is, to sell its use) for the limited period of time. If the land is rented, the rental will be that amount offered by the potential land-user having the highest reservation price for the use of the land over the limited period of time. If the land is sold, the sales price will be the highest offer received by the landowner for the use of the land over all future periods.

This then is the process by which the value of a piece of land is determined. The factors which determine this value, that is, the factors determining the reservation prices of the individuals involved, are very numerous.

In determining his reservation price, each potential user desiring the land for consumption purposes will be influenced by the prices of all other things on which he may spend his income, by the size of this income itself, by his set of tastes and preferences, and by the information which he possesses. This is the case because a change in any of these things will lead him to revise his budgetary decision. This, in turn, will alter the amount which he would be willing to pay to enjoy the use of the land, that is, his reservation price. Having altered his reservation price, he will thus have altered the amount which he will offer for the use of the land.

Similarly, each innovator must consider many factors in determining his reservation price for the use of the land. These will include the processes available for producing his product, the prices of other factors of production which he could use, and the perceived demand for his product. He must decide how much of his product to produce and which process to employ. The answer depends upon which of the processes is least expensive, and this depends upon the prices of the productive inputs which each process requires. Some processes require the piece of land in question, and others do not. Other things being equal, the innovator will be able to pay more for the piece of land and still have a productive process which requires it be the lowest-cost process available (and thus be employed) the lower are the prices of the other factors of production required for the same process which requires the land and the higher the prices of the factors of production required by alternative processes. He will also be able to pay more for the piece of land the greater the profits which he is able to obtain from his innovation, being, in effect, in the position of paying the landowner part of these profits for the use of the land. These profits will be strongly influenced by the demand for his product, and this will, in turn, be determined by all those things which determine the budgetary decisions of the individual households, namely, the set of goods and services available for them to buy, the prices of those goods and services, their incomes, their tastes and preferences, and the information they possess.

Finally, the reservation price of each speculator will depend upon what he believes he will be able to sell the land for in the future.

We have now examined those elements which determine the amount of income which can be obtained from entrepreneurial ability, from labor skills, and from a natural resource such as land. Let us now examine those elements which determine the amount available from capital.

Although the term capital has already been used a number of times in this book, it has not yet been clearly defined. What **is** capital? Why does it command an income? Essentially, capital is a surplus. It is that which is produced over and above that which is consumed. Capital consists, in the first instance, of a stock of consumable items, items such as food and clothing, which can sustain people while they are engaged in some activity other than that of producing for their own immediate needs. Capital is useful. It is useful because it sets people free from the continuing need to sustain themselves, thus enabling them to spend time producing items which magnify their ability to produce. Examples of such items are trucks, shovels, cranes, blast furnaces, in fact, any type of tool or building which facilitates and makes more efficient the productive process. These tools and buildings are themselves often referred to as capital equipment, capital goods, or as part of the "stock of capital," but they are not what we refer to here as capital. What we refer to as capital is a surplus of production or income above that which is consumed, and it is this surplus whose value we are now going to examine.

Households lend capital and entrepreneurs borrow it. This may sound strange at first since one does not usually think of himself as lending or borrowing spinach, wheat, milk, and tennis shoes. Nevertheless, that is what he is doing. When you loan someone a dollar, you are loaning him whatever that dollar will buy. He now has the money and will receive the goods and services, and you will not. Thus, the act of saving, that is, the act of creating a surplus of production above consumption, consists of releasing for others to consume items which you could have consumed but did not. It may seem that you are lending money, but you are lending capital. Furthermore, the interest rate which you receive for that money is really reflective of the usefulness of what that money will buy, specifically, the consumable items which sustain workers while they build the capital equipment which increases the ability of human beings to produce and satisfy their desires, thus increasing the stock of capital itself. In what follows, it will be useful to keep in mind this relationship between the money that is saved and lent and the capital which it represents.

Having thus defined capital as a surplus of production above consumption, it should be relatively easy to explain its value. To do so we need only examine the basic decisions of the individuals in the system, both as households and as entrepreneurs.

Each household makes a budgetary decision, and part of that decision is the matter of how much of its income to consume. It can either consume less than its current income, thereby adding to the stock of capital which it possesses, or it can consume more than its current income, thereby reducing its stock of capital. (It could do the latter, for example, by selling a bond and spending the receipts for consumption.) The decision as to how much to consume relative to current income is dependent upon a number of things which will be dealt with later on in our discussion. Suffice it for now to say that it is dependent upon the set of prices an individual confronts, the information he possesses, his wealth, and his set of tastes and preferences. In any case, each individual will elect to hold a specific stock of capital. Some of this capital will be held in the form of money, either as actual currency and coins or as the balance in a checking account. Another portion of his capital will be held in the form of durable goods such as houses, refrigerators, dishwashers, automobiles, and the like. At first glance the inclusion of items like these in one's stock of capital might appear strange. Upon further reflection, however, it seems more reasonable. When one buys an automobile, for example, he does not consume it. Rather, he consumes the flow of services which the automobile will yield him. The car itself is a fund of services, a stock of transportation, which can be drawn upon as its owner wishes. Furthermore, it remains intact and can be sold should he ever desire to use the capital which is embodied in it in some way other than for transportation. It will, of course, deteriorate with time, but so will a stockpile of clothing or canned peaches. A durable consumer good is properly thought of as capital and will be held by an individual whenever the flow of satisfactions which it yields him is greater than those yielded by the alternative assets he could hold, such as bonds or common stocks. These first two categories of an individual's capital assets have one thing in common. They both remain under the control of the individual who owns them. The third portion of his capital does not. This is the part which he elects to place at the disposal of others in return for an income stream. It is this portion which determines the value of capital.

In making his budgetary decision, each individual thus decides upon two things: first, how much to consume relative to his income and, second, the form in which to hold his resulting capital stock (that is, as money, consumer durables, or income-earning capital assets). In aggregate then, the set of all households decides to hold a certain quantity of each of these assets and, specifically for our present discussion, decides to lend out a specific quantity of capital in order to obtain an income stream.

Each entrepreneur must also make a decision regarding capital. In order to innovate he must have access to productive inputs such as labor skills, equipment, and raw materials, and these inputs must be paid for. Since these inputs will not be producing consumable products, being used instead to produce the productive facilities of the entrepreneur, their owners must depend for their subsistence upon consumable items produced but not consumed by others. That is, they must live on capital. The entrepreneur must thus obtain capital with which to obtain labor and materials with which to carry out his project.

How much will he borrow? His product can be produced by a number of processes. Each of these processes will require a specific bundle of labor, equipment, and materials, each of which costs a specific amount. One of these processes, he perceives, will yield him a future profit stream which he finds more attractive than that yielded by any other. This is the process he will select, and he will seek to borrow the amount of capital necessary to employ it. This is the amount of capital he will desire to borrow at the interest rate which he expects to prevail.

Borrowers and lenders will thus seek each other out. Each will be trying to strike the best bargain possible. Lenders will be seeking the maximum rate of interest, and borrowers will be seeking to pay the minimum. Lenders will seek the greatest possible assurances that their loans will be repaid, and borrowers will seek to furnish the least possible guarantee of that repayment. If the amount of capital which lenders desire to lend is in excess of the amount which borrowers desire to borrow, the borrowers will have the greater bargaining power. Whereas they will always be able to find another potential lender, the lenders will not all be able to find borrowers and will, consequently, be more willing than will borrowers to make bargaining concessions. As a result, the rate of interest will drift lower.

As the rate of interest declines, certain households will decide that the smaller income streams which their capital will now yield them are no longer sufficient to justify the sacrifices of other uses for it which the loans would require. These households will, therefore, decide to leave the market. Other (and presumably fewer) households will find that at the lower interest rate they must loan out greater amounts of capital in order to purchase future items which they are unwilling to forego. These households will thus increase the amount of capital which they seek to lend. Whether the amount of capital which households as a group seek to lend at the lower rate of interest will be greater or less than it was at the higher rate is not certain as it depends upon the relative abundance of the two types of households described above. The situation is somewhat more clear, however, where borrowers are concerned.

Those borrowers who are borrowing in order to increase their consumption will find that as the interest rate declines the sacrifice of future consumption which they must make in order to consume at the present time is reduced. Since they can now enjoy present consumption at a lower sacrifice, they can be expected to increase their borrowing. Those borrowers who are borrowing in order to undertake entrepreneurial activity will also increase their borrowing. They will do so for the following reason. Any given entrepreneurial activity will be undertaken if the stream of future expenditures it will require is sufficiently small relative to the stream of expected future income it will generate. Inasmuch as the stream of future expenditures will be larger the greater the amount which the entrepreneur must pay for the use of capital, as this amount declines certain investment projects will become profitable which were unprofitable at the higher interest rate. Consequently, as the interest rate declines, more and more investment projects will become attractive to entrepreneurs, and more and more entrepreneurs will seek to borrow the capital required to undertake them.

Hence, as the rate of interest declines the quantity of capital which individuals desire to borrow will increase, and the amount people desire to lend will probably either remain constant or decrease slightly. As this occurs, the bargaining power of borrowers will decrease relative to that of lenders, and the rate of interest will fall more slowly, stabilizing, in fact, once the relative bargaining power of the two sides reaches equality.

Other things besides changes in the rate of interest can also affect the amount of capital which people desire to borrow or to lend. On the lending side, the amount of capital available for borrowing will be influenced by those things that influence the makeup of the individual household budget. These would include, among others, the following. If households become pessimistic about the general economic outlook, they may become fearful that borrowers will be unable to repay their loans. If so, they will view the reward for making such loans as less attractive and will reduce the quantity of capital which they desire to lend. Changes in prices will also affect the amount of capital seeking a borrower. As the prices of goods and services change, the sacrifice required in order to loan a given sum of money will change as well. As this occurs, households will alter their budgets accordingly. As prices of productive factors change, the income and wealth positions of the households will be altered. Again, the budgets will be altered, presumably in the direction of increasing the amount of capital available for lending when the income of the household rises and reducing it when the income falls.

On the borrowing side, the quantity of capital desired will also be affected by things other than the rate of interest. Those people who borrow to consume decide on the quantity they wish to borrow as part of their general budgeting decision. Consequently, anything which affects this solution will affect the level of desired borrowing. These would include primarily the prices they face, their incomes, and their state of expectations about the future. If they expect future prices to be higher, they may decide to borrow and purchase now. If they expect their future incomes to be lower, they may reduce their borrowing and get out of debt. If a good consumption opportunity comes along, they may decide to borrow to take advantage of it.

Those people who borrow for entrepreneurial activity will also be influenced by a number of things. Any given investment project will be undertaken if the stream of expected future revenues it produces is high enough relative to the stream of expected future expenditures it requires. Consequently, anything which either reduces the stream of expenditures or increases the stream of expected revenues will increase the likelihood that a given project will be undertaken (thereby increasing the amount of capital sought by borrowers) and vice versa for anything having the opposite effect. As we have already seen, one of the things which affects the relative size of these two streams is the rate of interest. An increase in the rate of interest increases the expenditure stream, thus reducing the likelihood that a project will be undertaken. The expenditure stream will also be influenced by the prices of labor skills, equipment, and raw materials. The lower these prices, the less capital must be borrowed in order to undertake a project, and the smaller the expenditure stream will be. On the revenue side, the key word is expectations. The more optimistic the entrepreneur, the greater the revenue stream will appear, and the more likely he will be to innovate (and, thus, to borrow). Thus, anything which improves the general outlook for business will cause an increase in the demand of entrepreneurs for capital.

In addition to those factors determining the general outlook for business, the expected revenue stream will also be affected by the state of knowledge. Any new discovery which makes possible (or appears to make possible) a significant enough increase in the revenue which can be produced with a given amount of capital will lead entrepreneurs to innovate, and thus to borrow capital. Examples of such discoveries would be new products, new productive processes, new methods of organizing and managing a business enterprise, and the like. Thus, the value of capital is determined in part by what you can do with it.

The rate of interest is thus determined by the bargaining of those desiring to borrow and those desiring to lend. It will be influenced by all of the factors mentioned, and it will move in favor of those with the greatest bargaining power.

Having completed our discussion of those things which determine the returns to the skills, natural resources, entrepreneurial ability, and capital which households possess, we are now ready to conclude our discussion of how patterns of consumption are determined by the economic process. The conclusion is simple and undramatic. Each household is able to consume whatever it is able to pay for. Its income is determined by the assets which it elects through the budgetary process to place at the service of others and the value of the services of those assets as determined in the context of bargaining between those who want to provide them and those who want to use them. Thus, in order to enjoy a high level of consumption, a household must either possess assets whose services are valued very highly by others or else it must be successful as an entrepreneur.

The Invisible Hand

In the previous section, we had a rather lengthy discussion concerning the way in which the questions "Which items are produced?", "How are they produced?", and "Who consumes them?" are answered through the working of the economic process. You are now ready for one of the most important insights in economics, an understanding of and an appreciation for the phenomenon originally referred to by Adam Smith as the "Invisible Hand."

As was mentioned earlier, an economy is essentially a set of individuals. Each of these individuals possesses certain assets and seeks to use them to satify his desires as best he knows how. Each works as a highly specialized component of the overall division of labor. **No one is in charge.** No one tells an entrepreneur what to produce. No one tells a worker where to work or what skills to acquire. And yet there exists a degree of harmony in the economy as a whole which is really quite remarkable. Somehow or other just about the right amount of wheat is produced each year, just about the right number of size 9 1/2 shoes are made, just about the right number of toasters are manufactured and repaired. What at first may seem a rather chaotic state of affairs in which each individual goes his way quite without regard to what others are doing is actually a very orderly, in fact a profoundly orderly, process. It is a process which is sufficiently orderly that it coordinates the activities of millions of separate individuals, most of whom are completely unaware of the wants and desires of others or, indeed, of even their very existence. It is a process which produces among these millions of households a pattern of specialization, a division of labor, so complete that some individuals are able to live at a level of consumption unheard of a century ago and do nothing more than inspect bottles on an assembly line, spray for cockroaches, or teach Hindi to college students. It is a process guided by an invisible hand, and it operates as follows.

Each household has some assets and some desires. It also has an economic problem. In order to solve its economic problem, it prepares a budget, either explicitly or by default. Its budget is oriented toward the future in which the results of all its actions will become known. Because it is oriented toward the uncertain future, the budget of each household is based upon the expectations of that household as to its income, the prices of the things it will buy and sell, the demands of other households for the products it might produce, and so forth.

The budgets of the households are not consistent with each other. This is because no two households hold identical expectations as to the future and, consequently, no two households base their budgetary decisions upon the same set of assumptions. This being the case, it is not possible for all households to actually put their budgets into effect, that is, to actually employ their assets as their budgets indicate that they intend. Nonetheless, this is exactly what they try to do. Each household goes into the market intending to purchase a certain amount of each product and to sell a certain amount of each factor of production at the prices they expect to prevail. Each household seeks out trading partners and proceeds to bargain. As they do this, prices begin to change. If the number of bicycles of a certain type which people desire to purchase exceeds the number which they desire to produce, the price of these bicycles will drift upward as the prospective buyers bid against each other for those bicycles which are available. If the number of hours of barbering skill which people desire to provide exceeds the number which they desire to utilize, then the wages of barbers will decline as the sellers of this skill give way in the bargaining process and offer to provide their services for less. Thus, in the market for each product and for each factor of production the price will either remain steady, it will rise, or it will decline. But this movement of prices changes household expectations. Each household comes to realize that relative prices are not what it had expected them to be, and it alters its expectations accordingly. Based upon the new set of expectations, each household then revises its budgetary decision and tries to put the revised version into effect. Once again, however, this will be impossible. The future is still uncertain. It is true, of course, that more is known than was known before, but many things will also have changed. New innovations will have been made. Certain individuals will have changed their tastes and preferences. New resources will have been discovered, and old ones will have been exhausted. Therefore, as households attempt to put their revised budgets into effect, inconsistencies will once again manifest themselves, and the drift in relative prices will be altered. But this will again alter household expectations, household budgets, relative price movements, and so on *ad infinitum*. The process is endless. Households budget, prices change, households rebudget, prices change again, and so forth. Households never quite come into perfect harmony. This cannot occur as long as the future remains uncertain. But they do achieve a high degree of harmony. Whenever people want to buy more of an item than they want to sell of it, its price moves higher. As it does so, people revise their budgets, and the quantities they desire to buy and sell move closer together. Prices act as signals. They signal to households that information on relative scarcities necessary to enable each houshold to act in such a way that, while it is doing the best it can to satisfy its own desires, it is at the same time taking actions which are harmonious with those of the other households in the economy (although not perfectly harmonious as we have seen). **It is the movement of prices that coordinates the economic process**, and it is this set of freely-moving prices, each containing information about the opportunities facing the households, which constitutes the invisible hand. It is a "hand" because, like the hand moving a chessman, it leads each individual household to act in a way which is harmonious with the actions of others, and it is "invisible" because the household doesn't realize it is being led. Through the mechanism of the invisible hand, the high degree of coordination among households comes about which is necessary for the extreme division of labor upon which our standard of living depends, while, at the same time, each household is left free to choose for itself how its assets should best be employed.

The Cyclical Nature of the Economic Process

The economic process does not proceed smoothly. Instead, it is characterized by alternating periods of high economic activity in which nearly all of the productive skills and equipment in the economy are engaged in production and periods of low activity in which a relatively large proportion of these inputs remain idle. The former periods are often referred to as booms or periods of general prosperity while the latter periods are usually called recessions or (prior to 1930) depressions. An understanding of this cyclical movement in economic activity will be of immense importance to you as you endeavor to increase the value of your stock of assets, and it is the purpose of this section to provide **the basis** for such an understanding. **A fuller understanding must await our discussion of the role of government in the economic process.** Our discussion will proceed as follows. First, we will introduce some new definitions. Second, we will describe the nature of the flow of inputs, outputs, and money within the economic system. Third, we will digress briefly to consider some important aspects of money. Finally, we will examine the cycles themselves and the forces which shape them and will describe their principle features. Again, let me emphasize that the present discussion will be incomplete, ignoring as it will the role played by government, and that a more complete understanding will come later in Parts II and III, (especially on pages 82-90 and 101-104). **This point is very important** since the initial discussion, if taken by itself, would not describe the world in which you live **and may even do more harm than good.** Why then do we engage in it? It is necessary to proceed in this somewhat curious manner because while the modern business cycle cannot be understood without an understanding of the role of government, the role of government cannot be understood without first understanding how the cycle would operate in the absence of significant government activity. **With this warning clearly in mind**, let us proceed.

The Circular Flow

In Part I of this book, we discussed the process of budgeting. Through that process, each household was seen to allocate to specific uses its time, its capital, its natural resources, and its income. Consider the last of these, the allocation of income. A household's income can be allocated in a number of different ways. It can be used to purchase items like groceries, gasoline, or medical care for immediate consumption. It can be used to purchase items like clothing which are consumed over a slightly longer period of time. It can be used to purchase items like automobiles and furniture which are consumed over a longer period, or houses which are consumed over a still longer period. Finally, it can be stored in some form, presumably for consumption over an even longer period. For purposes of our current discussion, we will use the following definitions. Expenditures for items which are to be consumed in a relatively short period of time, such as those for groceries, clothing, or recreation, we will call **consumption spending.** (The actual period of time chosen is somewhat arbitrary, but it is not crucial to what follows.) All other allocations of a household's income we will define as constituting that household's **savings.** (Note that a clear distinction should be made between "savings" as defined here and the balance in the household's "savings account." The former is a flow concept [the amount of income the household receives less the amount it spends for consumption during a given **period** of time] while the latter is a stock concept [a portion of the household's stock of capital as measured at a given **point** in time]. A similar distinction should be made between "business savings" [as defined below] and the balance in the firm's "savings account".) Of those uses of income falling within a household's savings category, we will denote all except additions to its holdings of currency, noncollectible coins, checking account balances, and savings account balances as constituting its **investment**. Thus, a household's investment would consist of additions to its holdings of such things as bonds, common stocks, rare stamps and coins, houses, and automobiles. That portion of a household's savings which is not part of its investment will be defined as its **net savings**. A household's net savings thus consists of additions to its holdings of currency and noncollectible coins and additions to its checking account and savings account balances.

Consider next the household's allocation of capital. As you recall from our previous discussion, capital can be held in a variety of forms such as cash, automobiles, rare paintings, and common stocks. We are now going to divide these ways of holding capital into three categories. These categories are **money holdings** (consisting of holdings of currency and noncollectible coins and of checking account balances), holdings of "**near money**"(consisting of the balances of savings accounts), and **Type III capital assets** (consisting of all other ways of holding a household's capital).

In addition to the allocatory decisions comprising the household budget, another set of allocatory decisions are also of interest to us at this point. These are the allocatory decisions made by entrepreneurs as managers of their enterprises. Each business enterprise receives revenue. Part of this revenue will be paid to households and to other firms in return for the labor, equipment, and materials which they provide for the productive activity of the firm in question or to pay the living expenses of the entrepreneur. The remainder may be used to increase the productive capability of the firm (by, for example, purchasing more productive equipment) or to make investments in other firms (by, for example, purchasing common stock in another firm), or it may be held by the firm either in the form of cash, checking account balances, or savings account balances.

For our purposes we will employ the following definitions. These definitions are for the sake of convenience only and **do not necessarily correspond** to any accepted accounting terminology. (You will, of course, want to become familiar with accounting terminology before making any actual investments, but it is unnecessarily technical for present purposes.) **Business savings** will be defined as the firm's receipts each period minus its expenditures for the labor, equipment, and materials used to carry on current production and the amount taken out of the firm by the entrepreneur for his own personal use. **Business investment** will be defined as the firm's expenditures to increase its own productive capability plus its investments in other firms. **Net business savings** will be defined as business savings minus business investment. Net business savings thus consists of revenues allocated by the firm as additions to its holdings of cash, its checking account balances, or its savings account balances. Net business savings can, of course, be either positive or negative depending upon the relative sizes of business investment and business savings. Holdings of money, near-money, and Type III capital assets by business firms can be defined in a manner analogous to that used to define these holdings by households. That is, **holdings of money by a firm** would be the sum of its cash holdings and the balance of its checking accounts, **holdings of near-money by a firm** would be the balance of its savings accounts, and **holdings of Type III capital assets by a firm** would be the remainder of its capital assets, consisting of items such as machinery, common stocks, and the like.

Our definitions thus far relate only to the budgets of single households and single firms. By making some additions over all households and over all firms in the economy, however, we may define the following.

Aggregate consumption: The sum of the consumption expenditures of all the individual households.

Aggregate household savings: The sum of the savings of the individual households.

Aggregate household investment: The sum of the investment expenditures of the individual households.

Aggregate net household savings: The sum of the net savings of the individual households.

Aggregate money holdings by households: The sum of the money holdings of the individual households.

Aggregate holdings of near-money by households: The sum of the holdings of near-money of the individual households.

Aggregate holdings of Type III capital assets by households: The sum of the holdings of Type III capital assets by the individual households.

Aggregate business savings: The sum of the savings of the individual business firms.

Aggregate business investment: The sum of the investment expenditures of the individual business firms.

Aggregate net business savings: The sum of the net business savings of the individual firms.

Aggregate money holdings by firms: The sum of the money holdings of individual firms.

Aggregate holdings of near-money by firms: The sum of the individual firm holdings of near-money.

Aggregate holdings of Type III capital assets by firms: The sum of the individual firm holdings of Type III capital assets.

Aggregate savings: Aggregate household savings plus aggregate business savings.

Aggregate investment: Aggregate household investment plus aggregate business investment.

Aggregate net savings: Aggregate net household savings plus aggregate net business savings.

Aggregate money holdings: Aggregate money holdings by households plus aggregate money holdings by firms.

Aggregate holdings of near-money: Aggregate holdings of near-money by households plus aggregate holdings of near-money by firms.

Aggregate holdings of Type III capital assets: Aggregate holdings of Type III capital assets by households plus aggregate holdings of Type III capital assets by firms.

Having completed the foregoing (and, I'm afraid, rather tedious) definitions, we are ready to examine once again the manner in which households are related to one another in the economic process. We are ready to examine what is usually called the **circular flow**. This phenomenon operates as follows.

Each household endeavors to solve its economic problem. In doing so, it allocates its assets via the budgeting process so as to receive an income composed of rent for part of its natural resources, interest for part of its capital, wages for part of its time, and profits from its entrepreneurial activity. Each household then allocates each dollar of this income to either consumption, investment, or net savings. Those dollars allocated to consumption expenditures flow from the households to the business enterprises of the entrepreneurs (hereinafter referred to as "firms") in return for the products (including both goods and services) consumed. Those dollars allocated to investment expenditures flow either to firms or to other households. Expenditures for a bond, a share of stock, a rare coin, in fact any Type III capital asset previously owned by another household flow to that other household in return for the asset. Expenditures for a newly-created Type III capital asset such as a new house, a newly-issued bond, a newly-minted gold coin, or a new automobile, flow to the firm which produced the asset. Finally, those dollars allocated to net savings flow to a financial intermediary or are physically retained by the household. Additions to the household's checking account balance would flow to a "commercial bank" (defined as a financial intermediary which offers checking accounts). Additions to its holdings of near-money (that is, additions to the balance of its savings accounts) would flow to a financial intermediary which offers such accounts, such as, for example, a savings and loan association. Additions to its holdings of cash (that is, currency and noncollectible coins) would simply accumulate in the cookie jar or wherever else such holdings are kept.

Each business firm also receives an income. This consists of the revenue it receives for the goods and services it produces plus the amount it receives from the sale of newly-issued stocks and bonds. Part of this revenue flows back to the households in return for the labor, capital, and natural resources which they furnish the firm. Part flows to other firms in return for equipment or other productive inputs obtained from them. What remains is either retained by the firm as net business saving (either as cash in the firm, in checking accounts at commercial banks, or in savings accounts), invested in other firms, or returned to the households as their returns from entrepreneurial activity.

There is thus a flow, a circulation if you prefer, which characterizes the economic process. Factors of production flow from households to firms where they are transformed into finished products. These products then flow back to the households where they are consumed. Reflecting this flow is a reverse-flow of money. Consumption expenditures and household investment expenditures flow from households to firms as payment for consumption items and newly-created Type III capital assets, respectively, and rent, wages, interest, and profit flow back from firms to households as payment for the natural resources, labor, capital, and entrepreneurial effort which they provide. This flow of money is the circular flow, and it is very important for an understanding of the economic process.

The most important thing to note about the circular flow is this: all household income which does not become aggregate net household savings returns to the firms, and all the revenue of firms which does not become aggregate net business savings returns to the households. Thus, we may think of all expenditures by either households or firms as either "remaining in the flow" or as constituting "leakages" out of the flow (to commercial banks or to other financial intermediaries) as part of aggregate net savings. Of course, if aggregate net savings are negative (that is, if aggregate investment exceeds aggregate savings) then these negative net savings would constitute an addition of new expenditures to the circular flow from the commercial banks or other financial intermediaries from which the money spent was either borrowed or withdrawn. It is useful to think of the flow of spending as being much like a stream of water being pumped around a circular pipe from which some water is leaking and to which new water is being added. So long as the amount of water leaking out of the pipe is balanced by an equal amount of new water being added to the pipe, the amount of water flowing through the pipe will remain constant. Whenever the leakages exceed the additions of new water the volume of water flowing through the pipe will decline, and whenever the additions of new water exceed the leakages the volume of the flow will increase. In the same way, whenever the level of aggregate savings exceeds the level of aggregate investment, there exists a net leakage of spending out of the circular flow to the financial intermediaries and the volume of spending in the flow declines. Whenever the reverse is true the volume of spending in the flow increases. Now (assuming for the moment that there is no inflation in the system) the volume of spending in the circular flow is a measure of the level of economic activity in the economy as a whole. We will refer to it here as the **level of aggregate income.** (This term should not be confused with terms such as Gross National Product or National Income which frequently appear in the news. While such terms are also measures of aggregate economic activity, they have complex technical definitions which need not concern us here). Thus, whenever aggregate net savings is positive, the level of aggregate income is decreasing, and whenever aggregate net savings is negative, the level of aggregate income is increasing. Only if aggregate net savings were zero would aggregate income remain constant.

Armed with a basic understanding of the circular flow and of the important relationship between aggregate net savings and aggregate income, we are almost ready to discuss the business cycle. Before doing so, however, it will be useful to have a very short discussion about money. More specifically, you need to know what money is, where it comes from, and how its quantity relates to the circular flow.

A Short Digression on Money

As explained early in Part II of this book, the division of labor is a very important aspect of modern economic life. Through the process of each individual specializing and becoming expert in a narrow range of productive activities, it is possible for all to enjoy standards of living incomparably greater than what they could provide for themselves in isolation. But the division of labor requires exchange, and exchange can be cumbersome. Each individual must locate another individual who is willing to trade, and it may be difficult, for example, for someone who specializes in the production of toothpicks and who desires salt to find someone who specializes in the production of salt and desires toothpicks. It may be even harder for the specialist in the teaching of macrame to find a taxi driver willing to trade a ride in his cab for some macrame instruction. It may, of course, be possible for the macrame instructor to find someone who was willing to exchange, perhaps, typing services for macrame instruction and then find a cab driver who would trade a cab ride for the typing services, but, as is obvious, this would be very cumbersome. Too much time and effort would be taken up in making the intricate transactions required, and too little would remain for the production of goods and services for consumption.

Fortunately, the difficulties described above do not exist in a modern economy. This is because of the existence of **money.** What is money? Money is a commodity which is universally acceptable, that is, a commodity which every individual will accept in exchange for the goods and services which he produces. He will accept it not because he wants to consume it but because he believes that he will readily be able to exchange it for things which he does want to consume. If the macrame instructor has some money, she may trade it for the cab ride, and the cab driver can then trade the money for anything he wants to consume.

What sort of commodity can serve as money? First, the commodity should be hard to reproduce. If the monetary commodity were easy to reproduce, then it would soon require a very great deal of it to make exchanges, and moving and storing it would become difficult. Second, the money should be easily divisible to facilitate trades involving various amounts of the products desired. Third, money should be easily recognizable, for if someone does not recognize it as money they may refuse to accept it. Fourth, it should be relatively durable since any item subject to rapid deterioration would soon become unacceptable and useless for trading purposes.

Money, being a commodity, must be stored when not desired for immediate transactions. Inasmuch as theft is always a possibility, a set of individuals has arisen which specializes in satisfying the desire of people for a safe place to store their money. These individuals are the bankers. Bankers provide a storage service for which their customers are willing to pay a price. Why then do banks pay you interest on money which you deposit with them? They do this because, as they discovered long ago, it is not necessary for them to actually store the money for you at all. All that is required is that they be able to return your money to you when you desire it. Furthermore, since all units of money are interchangeable, it is not even necessary that they give you back the same units of money which you left with them. Due to the fact that only a small proportion of depositors will normally want to withdraw their money on any given day, bankers are able to operate with only a fraction of the money which has been left with them actually present at the bank and available to pay those individuals who do want to make withdrawals. This money which is available to pay off depositors will be referred to as the banks' **reserves.** Now bank reserves may be divided into two categories. Those reserves which the banker feels he must retain in order to meet anticipated withdrawals we will denote as **required reserves.** Any reserves which he holds in excess of his required reserves we will refer to as **free reserves.** (The terms required reserves and free reserves have been chosen as a matter of convenience and should not be confused with similar terms which often appear in the financial literature. These latter terms have somewhat technical definitions which need not concern us here.) With this understanding of the meaning of free reserves, we are now ready to discuss the process of money creation.

The quantity of money in the economy is not a constant thing. If you were to examine a statistical series on the quantity of money, such as those contained in the **Economic Report of the President,** you would find that it changes frequently. While the statistics are not gathered often enough to reflect this, the quantity of money changes hour by hour during every business day. It both increases and decreases. Furthermore, it does so in a manner which cannot possibly be related to the production of any physical commodity such as gold, currency, or coins. How can this be? What makes the money supply fluctuate?

The process by which money is created and by which it disappears operates as follows. Suppose a given commercial bank possesses free reserves. These reserves are money which the banker need not hold against withdrawals and for which he could receive interest were he to lend it out. (Note that we have now referred several times to the reserves of commercial banks as money. This was done only to smooth the flow of the discussion. In fact, such reserves are not considered part of the money supply which we define here as consisting of currency and coin held outside commercial banks plus the balances of checking accounts. Other definitions of the money supply also appear in the business and economics literature, but to consider them here would add little but complexity to our discussion.) Now suppose that a prospective borrower appears who meets all of the banker's criteria concerning honesty and general credit worthiness and who is willing to pay the rate of interest which the banker is asking. The banker will make the loan. In doing so, he will create a new checking account for the borrower on which he is free to write checks. Now checks are money. The vast majority of transactions take place through the use of checks. Checks are instructions by the depositor to the bank to pay the person to whom the check is written a specific quantity of money, currency and coin if that is what they desire. Checks are thus widely acceptable and meet the requirements of a monetary commodity. Thus, by creating a new checking account the banker has increased the supply of money in the economy. Everyone else still has all the money that they had before, and the borrower has more. There is, thus, more money. So long, therefore, as (1) banks possess free reserves and (2) there exist acceptable individuals who wish to borrow, loans will be made, and the money supply will increase. The money supply contracts by the reverse process. If a borrower repays his loan, then his checking account is extinguished. No one else has any more money than they had before. The bank has increased free reserves, but these do not add to anyone's purchasing power unless they are borrowed. Each depositor can spend whatever he has in his account, but he could have done that whether the bank possessed the extra free reserves or not. Thus, the repayment of loans without offsetting new borrowing results in a reduction in the money supply.

This then is the process by which the size of the money supply is altered, why it increases in some years and decreases in others. An understanding of this process should also improve your understanding of what takes place in the circular flow. Recall that money can "leak out" of the circular flow by being deposited in a checking account or a savings account. This money remains in the financial intermediary until borrowed (or else withdrawn by depositors). Once borrowed (or withdrawn), it returns to the flow as it is spent. What happens, however, if the amount that households and business firms desire to borrow exceeds the amount they desire to save? What happens, in other words, if aggregate net savings is negative? It was stated earlier that this results in the addition of new spending to the circular flow. But where does the money for this new spending come from? Some of it may, of course, come from withdrawals as depositors spend the balances in their accounts. Since, however, the set of individuals who are doing the investing are normally not the same set who previously did the saving, much of the money for the new spending is created in the commercial banks. So long as these banks possess free reserves, borrowers will be able to obtain loans, and the amount of money which is available for spending will increase. This is the primary means by which increases in the size of the circular flow (that is, increases in the level of aggregate income) are financed.

The process also works in reverse. When aggregate investment is less than aggregate savings, then loans from commercial banks are very likely being repaid faster than new loans are being made. In this case the repaying borrowers are losing the purchasing power represented by their checking accounts, and no one else is gaining it. Consequently, aside from those funds which merely accumulate in checking and savings accounts, the money which is "leaking out" of the circular flow as aggregate income declines is ceasing to exist.

As a final point in this digression on money, we should emphasize that the process of money creation and destruction only occurs in commercial banks, that is, in those financial intermediaries which offer checking accounts. This is because the holder of a checking account can spend the entire balance of that account at any time he chooses while the holder of a savings account cannot. Before the latter can spend the balance of his account he must withdraw his funds, and he cannot do that on demand unless the bank has sufficient reserves to permit this. He may be forced to wait a certain period of time in order to get his money. Thus, when someone places money in a savings account he has, in fact, less money than he had before. He has just as much **wealth,** but he would have had just as much wealth if he had bought a corporate bond or any other Type III capital asset. When, therefore, someone borrows from a financial intermediary which only offers savings accounts (such as a savings and loan association) the money he obtains is merely that given up by those who make deposits in that institution. When, on the other hand, someone borrows from a commercial bank, the money he obtains was not given up by the depositors with checking accounts. They can still spend all they could before, and he can spend more. Thus, the money supply has increased. Since this process requires that the institution involved offer checking accounts, it can only take place in commercial banks. Thus, the actual point at which new money originates to enter the circular flow, or where it vanishes after having left, is the set of commercial banks.

The Process of Economic Development

Have you ever visited Williamsburg, Virginia? As you are likely well aware, this colonial capital of Virginia has been painstakingly restored and today presents the modern visitor with as good a glimpse of life in the 18th century as can, I suppose, be gained anywhere. A visit to Williamsburg is most enlightening, as once one gets over being charmed by the candlelight in the old statehouse, the long dresses of the hostesses, and the spectacle of the horse-drawn carriages and military parades, he can't avoid being struck by the incredibly crude standard of living those people actually enjoyed. As the best form of transportation was by horse-drawn carriage, all travelers would arrive covered with either mud or dust, depending on the season. Each bedroom had bedwarmers indicating the type of heat provided by the many fireplaces, each of which had to be continually fed with firewood in the winter. There is not an indoor toilet in all of Williamsburg except for those maintained for visitors and employees. Rather, there is an ample collection of chamber pots which could be used at night or in bad weather and then emptied and cleaned at one of the outside toilets. When one goes into an 18th century kitchen, however, is when he gets the full flavor of life in the colonial era. All cooking was done before an open fireplace or in an oven which was built into the fireplace itself. Refrigeration did not really exist, so meat had to be smoked. Ice could be had during the summer months, however, if one took the precaution of cutting it from frozen lakes in winter and storing it in specially-built ice houses. Water was normally carried from a nearby well or stream.

Williamsburg is somewhat unique in that it features actual practitioners of crafts which are for the most part long forgotten. One of these is paper-making according to 18th century methods. We didn't actually see the entire process, missing the gathering and processing of the rags into pulp, but what we did observe, the actual making of sheets of paper, was very interesting. The sheets of paper were made one at a time. A square, framed screen was dipped into a solution containing the pulp and, after becoming coated with this substance, was allowed to dry in the sun.

When dry, the sheets of paper were taken next door to the print shop where they were converted into souvenirs for visitors to purchase. The printing was again done one sheet at a time. This was, of course, a considerable improvement over the earlier practice, which was to print one letter at a time by hand. It is just as well that very few could read at that time as you can imagine how much a hand-written book must have cost.

We visited many other shops as well. Among these were a bakery in which the baker spent about 20 minutes rolling out an immense blob of dough out of which a second baker cut cookies (as I recall, his rolling pin did not have handles on the ends), a musical instrument shop in which the craftsmen talked in terms of weeks to make individual guitars, and a flour mill which was powered by a large windmill. All of the craftsmen in these shops wore very plain-looking shirts and kneebritches.

Don't misunderstand. We enjoyed very much our visit to Williamsburg, and to the neighboring settlement of Jamestown as well, and we admired greatly the skill of the artisans who labored in the ancient arts. But when all is said and done, it cannot be denied that the colonial inhabitants of Williamsburg lived very short and very hard lives by present-day standards. This is especially clear when one realizes that nearly all of the structures which have been preserved from those days were either commercial or state buildings or belonged to the very well-to-do citizens. The average man simply didn't have the time to do all of the things necessary to live the life which we are wont to associate with colonial days. He spent nearly all his time in the field, milking the cows, feeding the horse or chickens, or fixing the farm implements. Meanwhile, his wife was busy making butter, making candles, keeping the fire going, washing clothes on a scrubbing board, or spinning yarn from which to weave cloth later on.

I have engaged in this fairly extended description of life in colonial America for a reason. That reason is to point out that, measured by any standard you want to use except possibly room to move around, the material standard of life today is vastly greater than it was in the 18th century. It is also greater than it was in the 19th century, in the early 20th century, and even somewhat greater than it was 10 years ago.

Why do you suppose that this is the case? Is it because we are better workers today? Is it because we are smarter? Clearly not. The artisans of Williamsburg were every bit as good at their trades as we are today at ours. Indeed, some of the greatest men in the history of this nation were frequent visitors to or even citizens of Williamsburg and its environs. No, men are not any better today. But they do possess a better technology.

What is technology? It is knowledge. It is knowing how to do things. It is knowing how to design a vehicle that will fly, how to build a railroad, how to make an antibiotic. It is knowing how to make a furnace that will produce 300 tons of steel in 20 minutes, an oven that will bake 600,000 crackers an hour, or a press that will print hundreds of thousands of (very thick) newspapers every day. That is what technology is, and it is the **only** thing that separates us from the citizens of Williamsburg, or from the citizens of Stonehenge for that matter, where standard of living is concerned. It is not that we have any more intelligence. It is just that we have had a longer time to discover things and to put them to practical use.

Now the process by which technology improves through time is the process of innovation. It is the process which we discussed earlier when we were considering the entrepreneur. Someone has an idea. He thinks he sees a way in which existing factors of production, existing natural resources, labor skills, and capital, can be combined in a new way so as to produce something which has greater value than what they were producing before. He doesn't **know** that this will be the case, but if he has sufficient faith in his idea he will become an innovative entrepreneur. He will obtain the necessary skills, materials, and equipment and will put his idea to the test. If he is correct, he will have created value, much of which will accrue to him as profit. If he is wrong, he will have taken a loss. But there is more involved than that. If he is wrong, his idea will be quickly forgotten, and the world will be little the worse for his folly. If he is correct, however, he will have improved the technology and, thus, the standard of living of society as a whole. This is how technology improves through time. Through trial and error. Through trying one thing and then another. Enjoying success and riches or experiencing failure and ruin. It is the innovative entrepreneur who is primarily responsible for the rise in living standards throughout the whole of recorded history. There is a risk involved in improving a technology, the risk that you may be wrong and that the time, energy, and resources expended on the project will be lost. It is the entrepreneur who is willing to take this risk, and it is through his doing so that economic progress is made.

The process of innovation, or of economic development, does not proceed smoothly, however. It moves in alternating waves of heavy innovative activity and very light innovative activity. It moves, in fact, in cycles.

The process of economic development moves in cycles because entrepreneurs are risk-avoiders. They are less prone to avoid risk than are non-entrepreneurs, but they are risk-avoiders, nonetheless. Being risk-avoiders, they are only willing to innovate when the risk involved in doing so appears acceptably small, and this condition is only met at certain points in time.

From time to time, economic conditions develop which are very favorable to innovative activity. These are periods when the probability of success appears especially great. The costs of the factors required for the project are relatively low, and the demand for the finished product appears relatively strong. These periods normally occur toward the end of other periods called **recessions**.

During recessions, people are pessimistic. Business is bad. Profits are low. Workers are losing their jobs as their employers find themselves unable to sell enough output to justify their continued employment. Very little innovative activity is undertaken during recessions, aggregate net savings is positive, and aggregate income declines.

As the recession continues, however, the mood of pessimism begins to change. This occurs primarily for three basic reasons. First, as the level of aggregate income declines, the level of aggregate savings declines even faster. As people's incomes decline, they reduce their level of consumption spending, but they reduce it less than proportionately to their reduction in income. A person who loses his job, for example, does not simply quit consuming. He can't. He must still eat, stay warm, and have medicine if he becomes ill. He will do what he can to reduce his expenditures, but they will not go to zero. Rather, he will live off his savings, he will resort to charity, or, if all else fails, he will resort to crime. He will consume something. If aggregate consumption declines more slowly in a recession than does aggregate income, then it follows that aggregate savings is declining more rapidly.

Recall now the dynamics of the circular flow which we discussed earlier. As long as aggregate net savings is positive, aggregate income will decline. When aggregate net savings is negative, aggregate income will increase. And the **speed** of the increase or decrease in aggregate income depends upon the size of aggregate net savings. Thus, if aggregate net savings is positive and large (that is, if aggregate savings is much larger than aggregate investment) then aggregate income will not only decline, but will decline faster than if aggregate net savings is positive but small (that is, if aggregate savings is only slightly larger than aggregate investment). Recall our analogy of water flowing through a pipe. If there is a large leak in the pipe the volume of water in the pipe will decline faster than if there is a small leak.

During a recession, aggregate investment is low. It is low throughout the recession. As aggregate savings declines, therefore, aggregate net savings declines as well, and the leakage of money out of the circular flow begins to close off. As aggregate net savings contracts, the rate of decline of aggregate income decreases. Consequently, as the recession proceeds, the rate of decline in the level of economic activity itself begins to decline. This is a hopeful sign. Declines in aggregate income are really not all that much fun, so a reduction in the rate of decline can't be anything but good news for the economy, and it, therefore, contributes to a lessening of the pessimistic mood which is characteristic of the recession.

The second reason why the pessimism of the recession comes to an end has to do with the prices of the factors of production—raw materials, labor skills and capital. Recall that the prices of these items are determined through the market process, that is, they are determined through bargaining between those individuals desiring to sell and those individuals desiring to buy. Whenever the quantity of a particular factor which people, in aggregate, desire to buy exceeds the quantity they desire to sell, the bargaining power will be on the side of the sellers, and price will move upward. When the reverse is true, price will decline. Now who are the buyers of the factors of production? They are the entrepreneurs. And why do entrepreneurs desire factors of production? They desire them to carry out innovations through which they hope to obtain profit. Consequently, whenever entrepreneurs believe that it is profitable to do so they will go into the market to purchase factors of production. They do not feel this way during recessions. During recessions, business is bad. Firms have trouble selling their products. Household incomes are falling so they are more reluctant to buy things. The outlook is, in a word, pessimistic. Since entrepreneurs are pessimistic along with everyone else, they do not innovate. They do not think it will be profitable to do so. Since they don't innovate, they don't require the services of the factors of production. They thus do not endeavor to purchase them, and the number of people desiring to sell these factors comes to greatly exceed the number desiring to buy. As this occurs, the bargaining power shifts to the side of the buyers and, since buyers never want to pay any more than necessary, prices drift downward. Thus, the prices of productive factors decline during the course of a recession. The reason why this leads to the end of the pessimism will become clear in a moment.

Finally, the third reason why the pessimistic outlook of the recession begins to fade has to do with history. The business cycle is inherent in the market process. Cycles have been repeating themselves for as long as anyone can remember. Thus, people expect the recession to end. No one knows, of course, **when** it will end, but the fact that all past recessions **have** ended leads people to believe that the present one will end as well. Thus, the third reason for the end of the pessimism is that people expect that the recession will ultimately end.

Now then, let's examine how these three causes interact to end the pessimism of the recession and, with it, the recession itself.

As noted previously, no one knows exactly when the recession will be over. There are, however, signs. In particular, there is the rate of decline in aggregate income itself. Because aggregate net savings falls faster during the recession than aggregate income, the leakage from the circular flow becomes smaller relative to the size of the flow, and the rate of decline of the flow declines. This is a signal that the leakage which caused the decline is closing itself off and that aggregate income will not fall as fast in the future. Since the amount that people will spend is positively related to their incomes, the news that income will not decline as rapidly in the future as in the recent past is taken as an optimistic signal, a signal making entrepreneurs more likely to innovate.

A second factor which improves the outlook for investment is the low level of input prices. Each entrepreneur, as he contemplates the desirability of an innovation, compares two things. On the one hand, he has the prospective stream of returns from his enterprise. On the other hand, there is the stream of expenditures necessary to produce that stream of returns. The smaller the stream of expenditures relative to the stream of returns, the more likely he will be to go ahead with the project. Consequently, as the recession draws toward its close, entrepreneurs become more and more likely to invest. Since the prices of labor, raw materials, and equipment are declining, less capital will be necessary to carry out any given investment project. This will mean a lower stream of expenditures. Furthermore, the interest rate will also likely be low, reducing the required expenditures even further.

As the stream of expected expenditures declines, the stream of expected returns will be increasing. When the recession began, the probability was that it would continue for some time. This made the expected returns from a typical investment project appear relatively low. As the recession proceeds, however, and as aggregate income begins to stabilize (that is, to fall less rapidly), the belief that the recession is ending causes this expected stream of returns to increase. While it was always assumed that the recession would end someday, the indication that its ending is imminent "moves up," so to speak, the expected date at which the returns from the project will actually be received and increases their prospective value at the date of decision. (Technically, we would say that it increases the **present value** of the stream of expected returns, but, this not being a book on investing, we need not get into the complexities of that rather useful concept here.) We thus have the expected expenditure stream declining and the stream of expected returns becoming more valuable. When, for any given project, these trends have gone far enough that the entrepreneur views himself as being better off if he innovates than if he does not innovate, he will take the plunge.

We are now ready to see the whole picture, how the pessimism of the recession is ended and the recovery begun. It is simply a matter of the three causes mentioned earlier working themselves out. As the recession continues, the rapid decline in aggregate savings and the recollection that previous recessions have ended combine to increase the values of the expected streams of returns to the various innovative projects. At the same time, the falling factor prices reduce the streams of expenditures required to proceed. As these trends continue, then, one-by-one, the projects of the various entrepreneurs appear to them as profitable and are undertaken. Thus, aggregate investment will begin to increase. It will increase slowly at first, the investment outlook still being relatively pessimistic and uncertain, but, as aggregate investment increases, aggregate net savings will decrease even faster than it was decreasing before. This will cause the fall in aggregate income to slow down even more, thereby further brightening the investment outlook. This new optimism will cause more projects to appear worth the risk, and more innovative activity will occur. Thus, it proceeds. As each entrepreneur innovates, his action causes the circular flow to be greater than it would otherwise have been, and this, in turn, leads other entrepreneurs to invest. The process is cumulative. It feeds upon itself. Through it, pessimism becomes optimism, the fall in aggregate income stabilizes and becomes an increase, and the recession gives way to the **recovery**.

We have now seen why it is that innovative activity tends to be clustered into certain periods of time, specifically, those periods which begin very late in recessions and extend through the subsequent recovery and most of the following boom. In order to see this more clearly, let's examine the contrasting periods, those in which the level of innovation nearly disappears. To do this, we merely proceed on through the remainder of the cycle.

The recovery is the name we will give to the period during which the general outlook changes from the pessimism of the recession to the optimism of the period which follows which we shall call the boom. What occurs during the recovery is simply that, in steadily growing numbers, entrepreneurs become convinced that the time is right for innovation and go ahead with their projects. As they do so, the level of aggregate net savings becomes negative, and its absolute level increases. This causes aggregate income to begin rising and then to rise at a steadily increasing rate. Since aggregate income is rising during the recovery, it must be that additional money is entering the circular flow. This additional money is coming both from the commercial banks where it is being created to finance the expansion in economic activity and from the other financial intermediaries where it has been idle. Each entrepreneur that decides to innovate must have capital for his project. To obtain this capital he must have money, and for this reason he goes to a commercial bank or to some other financial intermediary such as a savings and loan association or an insurance company. (If he borrows directly from households, the money he spends does not add to the circular flow unless it would have otherwise merely been placed in the mattress. It merely replaces the money that is not spent by the household that gives him the loan.) At the nonbank intermediaries, the money he borrows is money that has previously been left there by others. At the commercial banks, the money he borrows is new money which is created as the banks lend out their free reserves.

With their new spending power, the entrepreneurs go into the market to hire factors of production. As they do so, they constitute an addition to those desiring to buy these factors and, therefore, begin to shift the balance of bargaining power in favor if those who desire to sell. Thus, the prices of factors of production do not fall as rapidly as they had before, and they begin to stabilize. As factor owners begin to receive the relatively higher levels of wages, interest, and rents, they in turn increase their spending, which makes it easier for entrepreneurs to sell their products and further reinforces the optimistic outlook which is developing. This convinces even more entrepreneurs that it is a good time to invest, they borrow money and hire factors of production, the factor owners spend their new incomes, the sales of business firms again increase, and the optimism becomes stronger still.

Economic activity is largely a matter of expectations, and as the outlook becomes brighter, the optimism becomes contagious, affecting nearly everyone in the economy. As this occurs, the recovery blends imperceptibly into the **boom**.

During the boom, the outlook is one of optimism. Business is good. Sales are increasing. The sellers of labor skills, raw materials, equipment, and capital services find that they are more easily able to find buyers and, furthermore, that these buyers are not so hard to bargain with as they were during the recession. As a result, the incomes of factor owners increase, they become more confident of the future, and they begin to spend more freely, perhaps making purchases which were postponed during the previous recession. Entrepreneurs invest because the outlook is good, and the outlook is good because entrepreneurs invest. The whole process feeds upon itself, and the money supply expands to provide the financing to keep it going.

Thus, as the boom proceeds, factor prices rise, the prices of finished products rise as their producers are forced to pay more for the factors, the money supply is increasing, the number of unemployed workers is decreasing, the level of free reserves in the commercial banks is falling, and aggregate income is increasing. There is also an increase in the number of business enterprises as the wave of optimism persuades group after group of entrepreneurs to innovate.

But it cannot continue. Sooner or later, a period is reached which we will call the **crisis**.

The crisis is, roughly speaking, the reverse of the recovery. It is a period during which the optimism of the boom first fades and then becomes the stark pessimism of the recession which follows. As might be expected, the crisis is brought on by forces which are the reverse of those which bring about the recovery. Specifically, these are the tendency of aggregate savings to increase faster than aggregate income during the boom, the tendency of factor prices to rise, and the recollection that booms don't last forever.

During the boom, aggregate income increases. Factor prices increase, and more factors find employment. As aggregate income rises, aggregate consumption rises as well. The rise in consumption, however, is less than proportionate to the rise in income. People tend to be creatures of habit so far as their spending patterns are concerned. Further, they tend to base their consumption standards on what they perceive to be their long-run expected levels of income. Since they don't perceive the loss of their job to be a permanent thing, they don't fully adjust their level of consumption to such a temporary situation. Similarly, they don't greatly increase their consumption levels when they are rehired. The result of this is that aggregate consumption is more constant over time than is aggregate income. This implies that aggregate savings will be less constant than aggregate income. We have seen how this phenomenon operates during the recession to reduce the rate of decline in aggregate income and bring about the recovery. The same thing happens, in reverse, during the boom. As aggregate income rises, aggregate consumption rises as well but does so more slowly. Aggregate savings rises more rapidly, therefore, and must either be offset by a similar increase in aggregate investment or aggregate net savings will begin to increase, thereby causing a reduction in the rate of increase of aggregate income. During the early part of the boom such an increase in aggregate investment is indeed forthcoming, but, as we shall see, this changes as the boom proceeds.

During the boom, investment is high. Persuaded by the optimism which surrounds them, entrepreneurs innovate. As they do so, they hire more and more factors of production to build and operate their productive facilities. At first, there are large reserves of unemployed workers, high levels of free reserves in the commerical banks, and excess capacity for the production of raw materials and productive equipment. As time passes, however, and more and more innovation is undertaken, this situation changes. Unemployed workers become few in number. Bankers begin to run low on free reserves. Firms producing raw materials and equipment begin operating at near-capacity levels. In each case, the result is the same, a rise in factor price. As the buyers of factors increase relative to the factor suppliers, the balance of bargaining power shifts inevitably in favor of the latter. They are thus able to drive harder bargains, and factor prices drift upward.

Finally, as the boom gets longer and longer, people, looking back upon a history in which every boom has been followed sooner or later by a recession, begin to wonder how much longer it can last.

Throughout the boom, then, but especially after it has gone on for quite a while, the two all-important expected payment streams, the stream of expected returns from a given prospective innovation and the stream of expenditures needed to produce those returns, are moving. And they are moving in a direction unfavorable to innovation. The cost of factors is increasing, necessitating heavier borrowing in order to innovate. At the same time, the rate of interest is rising as bankers become progressively more reluctant to allow their reserves to decline below the low levels to which the heavy borrowing of the boom has driven them. This increases the cost of innovation as well. One by one, entrepreneurs observe the slowdown in the rate of growth of aggregate income brought about by the high and growing level of aggregate savings and conclude that the boom has about run its course. Translating this into a decline in the value of the expected income streams from their prospective projects, they decide in steadily increasing numbers that now is not a good time to invest. As the level of aggregate investment begins to falter and to fall nearer and nearer the rising level of aggregate savings, the flow of money into the circular flow steadily closes off causing the slowdown in the growth of aggregate income to become more noticeable. And, just as the reverse of this phenomenon had earlier led to the onset of the recovery, the progressive slowing in the growth of economic activity spreads growing concern among entrepreneurs. One by one, they decide to postpone investment projects and to get themselves into the more liquid financial positions which they know will be desirable should the recession which they begin to expect actually materialize. Borrowing at the banks is, thus, reduced, and the repayment of loans causes the money supply to grow at a slower rate or to begin to contract.

Again the process is cumulative. The more the boom slows down, the more investment is cut back, and the more investment is cut back, the more the boom slows down. The circles of pessimism spread wider and wider, investment slows to a trickle, and the recession has begun.

As noted earlier, the recession is a boom in reverse. The mood is pessimism. Investment is declining. This decline in investment, coming as it does in the context of the high level of aggregate savings carrying over from the preceding boom, causes the circular flow to shrink at a faster rate. Businesses cannot sell their existing levels of output and are forced to lay off workers and reduce their purchases of equipment and raw materials. As factor owners become more concerned about their futures, they reduce their levels of consumption, which in turn reinforces the impression that business is bad and that the time is not right for investment. Down go factor prices as factor suppliers compete against each other to serve the few buyers still in the market. Prices of finished products fall as well as their costs of production decline and their producers endeavor to maintain output and sales at levels as high as possible. In those industries where firms elect to maintain prices, the reductions in output and in factor employment are especially severe.

The recession, however, is not all bad. It has a bright side as well. While it may not appear so to those who are taking part, the recession is performing a truly useful service for society as a whole. It is performing what the late economist Joseph A. Schumpeter, to whom, incidentally, we owe much of the theory of the business cycle presented here, described as the process of **creative destruction**.

In order to understand the process of creative destruction, it is useful to refer again to something which occurred during the recovery and boom. As you recall, these were periods of optimism. Entrepreneur after entrepreneur went through the process of innovation. New enterprise after new enterprise was formed and went into business. Not only were new enterprises established, but old ones were expanded and modernized as well. In short, the productive capacity of the economy was greatly increased during the boom. At first, this was very good for business. Much of the innovative activity consisted of the construction of new facilities such as factories, stores, and equipment. The money paid to construct these facilities found its way into the purchase of goods and services from existing firms, and this added to the wave of optimism. Later on, as the new facilities were completed and started to produce, aggregate income was high and increasing. Households were optimistic and were spending freely, and very few firms had trouble in selling their outputs.

With the crisis, however, the situation changed. As aggregate income stabilized and began to decline, a chilly wave of pessimism began to spread throughout the economy. As households became more apprehensive about their future incomes, they began one by one to revise their budgetary allocations. Where optimism had led them to spend freely, pessimism had just the opposite effect. Austerity became the order of the day, and households began to pay closer attention to how they were spending their money, endeavoring wherever possible to avoid expenditures and make do without them. The effect on business was dramatic.

Whereas during the recovery and boom the rapidly expanding capacity of the economy had appeared justified by the steadily expanding level of aggregate income, the crisis brings a revelation. The level of capacity in many lines of production is too great to be sustained. Far more firms exist than can be operated profitably under the reduced spending patterns of the households. It is at this point that households decide which firms will survive and which firms will be destroyed. They do this by their budgeting decisions, that is, by deciding which products they really want to buy and which products they can do without. The innovations which took place during the recovery and boom are put to the test during the recession. Those which pass this test remain to profit from the following boom. Those which fail the test go bankrupt, and the labor skills, raw materials, and equipment which they were using are released, thus becoming available for the new enterprises which will spring forth in the new recovery. This is the process of creative destruction. It is destructive because it destroys many firms. It is creative because the firms which are destroyed are, for the most part, those producing those products least desired by households, and the factors of production released as they cease operations become available to produce more desirable products in the future. It is the process by which the stage is set for recovery and for the next cycle.

Thus, the cycle goes. Boom. Crisis. Recession. Recovery. Boom. Crisis. Recession. Recovery. The process is not regular in the sense that all cycles or stages of cycles are of equal, or even predictable, length. Many things can intervene to make a boom unusually long or a recession unusually severe. The major such factors would be external developments which provide exceptionally rich or poor innovative opportunities for the entrepreneurs. The discovery of vast new resource deposits, an unusual breakthrough in some field of scientific knowledge, or perhaps the coincidental occurrence of several such events (or their opposites) would be examples of developments which occur largely by chance and thus add a touch of randomness to the cyclical movements. While the cycle is thus neither regular nor easily predictable, it is a cycle just the same. Each boom is followed by a recession, and each recession is followed by a boom. Pessimism is followed by optimism, and optimism is followed by pessimism. It is inherent in the economic process, inherent, at any rate, whenever entrepreneurs are free to innovate in pursuit of profit.

This section was introduced with the heading "The Process of Economic Development," yet we have, for the most part, discussed the business cycle. How are the two related? They are very closely related in that the business cycle is a reflection of the process of innovation or economic development. It is the result of the innovative activity of entrepreneurs who avoid risk and have imperfect information about the future. It is inherent in the process through which development occurs. With each succeeding boom, new technology is introduced into the productive structure of the economy. With each succeeding recession, the households decide which technology is, indeed, superior. They then embrace this superior technology and discard the alternative. Thus, at the end of each succeeding cycle the economy is more productive, the standard of living is higher, than it was before. It is higher because the work of production is being carried out with better tools, in better ways, and with greater knowledge. The business cycle is a reflection of the process by which the economy moves, step by step, from Williamsburg to the present day. It cannot be removed so long as individuals remain free to pursue their images of happiness as they choose. Consequently, you should expect it to remain an aspect of economic life (although in the somewhat modified form which we will discuss below), and you should make your decisions accordingly.

The Visible Hand

If the economic process could be described by a single word, that word would have to be **dynamic**. It is constantly in motion. New resources are always being discovered. New products and new processes are always coming onto the market. Expectations and the tastes of households are always changing. Consequently, the demands for all products and productive factors are continually being altered, as are also the quantities which people desire to supply, and their prices are forever moving as households engage in the never-ending process of solving their economic problems. In short, everything is in a state of continual change and motion.

One implication of this dynamism is a high degree of uncertainty. Not only is everything changing, but it is changing in a way that cannot be predicted. Who can foresee the next major resource discovery? Who can foresee the next great invention? Since uncertainty exists, people must make guesses, and sometimes they guess wrong. Consequently, along with the production of goods and services, the economic process produces disappointment. It is characterized by insecurity.

Insecurity, however, is something which people dislike. People are risk-avoiders. They enjoy a high degree of certainty, a high degree of predictability in their enviroment. They want to be able to plan for the future. They want to be able to take actions which will assure that their desires will be met as they arise. They want, in a word, security.

Yet security is one thing that the economic process **cannot provide**. The reason for this is simple. All the activity of households is directed toward the future when the results of their current efforts are expected to materialize, and the future is uncertain.

All economic decisions must be made in the context of uncertainty. This is obvious in the case of the entrepreneur, but it is only slightly less true in the case of those who furnish the natural resources, the labor skills, and the capital needed for the productive process. Take, for example, the case of an artisan such as a watchmaker. The acquisition of this skill takes time and effort. It is expensive. The time and effort spent on learning how to repair watches could have been spent on something else. This time and effort constitutes an investment into acquiring the watchmaking skill. What, however, is the value of that skill? It depends on what people will pay for it, and, as we have already seen, this depends upon a large number of things, **virtually all of which are unknown to the artisan at the time that he decides to become a watchmaker**. It is the same for any skill. No one who makes an investment of time (or, for that matter, no one who makes an investment of money or who sells natural resources on credit) has any guarantee that he will be rewarded for that act—certainly no guarantee that his reward will match his expectations. Surprises occur. The development of the electronic wristwatch destroys the demand for repairmen of spring-powered watches. The invention of the internal combustion engine destroys the demand for mule skinners. The invention of the telegraph destroys the demand for pony express riders. What do you suppose would be the impact on the demand for dentists of a toothpaste which actually eliminated tooth decay?

Since the future is uncertain, all economic decisions must be made in the absence of complete information. They must all be made on the basis of assumptions about the existing state of the world. This is always the case. If one were to wait until he actually knew what the outcome of a course of action would be, the opportunity to take that course of action would have passed. To be sure, people try to get all the information that they can, but it is simply impossible to get **all** the relevant information. There are simply too many things to consider. Consequently, they act on the basis of assumptions about those things on which they have no information. This is correct. It is the correct way to make decisions. There is nothing that can be said in criticism of such an approach to decision-making since one should never go to the expense of gathering information the value of which does not appear to justify the effort. And yet it implies that from time to time the assumptions will prove incorrect in the wrong direction and that the result will be an unfortunate outcome—literally unfortunate. That is, it will be an outcome which resulted from nothing more than the bad **luck** of the decision-maker. It is thus entirely possible to approach all of one's decisions in exactly the right way and still experience undesirable outcomes. It is, of course, true that approaching one's decisions in the proper manner will reduce the probability of undesirable results, but the laws of probability only become relevant when large numbers of decisions are made. Since the number of major decisions which the typical household will make in a lifetime (decisions, that is, such as buying a business, choosing a trade, or making a major securities purchase) is quite small, it is entirely possible that a household can experience a low standard of living (be forced, that is, to settle for a low level of desire satisfaction) over its entire lifetime through sheer bad luck. This is especially likely when the outcome of its initial decision is adverse since it can take a long time to overcome a heavy capital loss.

What is the purpose of this extended discussion of the vagaries of economic life? How does this help you to understand the factors which determine value? The purpose is this. The facts that (1) the economic process is characterized by insecurity and (2) human beings desire security imply that human beings dislike the economic process as it has been described thus far. Up to this point, we have been describing a world in which government takes no significant part in economic affairs, acting merely as a disinterested keeper of the peace. Such a world has never existed, and it never will exist. Consequently, the theory of value described thus far is not revelant to the world in which you live. It can only be made relevant if we expand it to include a consideration of the role of government in the economic process and the consequences of this for the theory of value. It is the purpose of this section to provide such a consideration of the role of government, and it was the purpose of the discussion of the insecurity of the economic process to introduce our theory of government activity. This is the purpose of the discussion, as the introduction to an aspect of the economic process which is of immense importance (but which, incidentally, is normally ignored in economics courses).

To understand how the insecurity of the economic process gives rise to an active role for government, we need only examine the source of the insecurity. Some insecurity is apparently inevitable. Crops fail. Wars break out. Tastes change. Much of the insecurity in economic life, however, comes from a source which is not beyond human control. This source is the entrepreneur. It is the entrepreneur who innovates. It is the entrepreneur who introduces new products, develops new resource discoveries, and utilizes new processes. Since each of these innovations has an impact on the fortunes of each and every other entrepreneur and, thus, on the income of each and every household, they are a tremendous source of insecurity. The activities of entrepreneurs constitute a very real and serious threat to the well-being of all existing firms and to the immediate well-being of all those who supply them with labor skills, natural resources, and raw materials. They represent the threat of **competition**, and no one likes competition. (Competition with the other fellow is fine, of course, since it results in a greater range of choice for you, but competition with you is quite another matter.) The only way to avoid the insecurity caused by the entrepreneur is, thus, to prevent him from acting as an entrepreneur. But since he views it as being in his own interest to act as an entrepreneur, he will not refrain from doing so voluntarily. Consequently, preventing his acting as an entrepreneur requires the application of force, either actually or via threat. And it is the government which provides this force.

The Nature of Government

As mentioned in the preceding section, people desire security and predictability in their lives. A major ingredient of this security is a peaceful society, that is, the existence of law and order. Law and order can only exist, however, if someone can enforce the law. Thus, the existence of a peaceful society implies the existence of an agent who controls sufficient physical power—sufficient soldiers, rifles, tanks, or what have you—to "get its way." Such an agent is by definition unique. This agent may be called a chief, a king, an emperor, a dictator, a parliament, a legislature, or whatever, but its one essential characteristic is that it exercises control over a preponderance of the means of violence existing within the society. In what follows, we will refer to this agent as a **ruler**.

Note that the ruler only exercises control over the means of physical violence. They are not inherent within it. Rather, the means of violence are inherent in the citizens in varying proportions. One citizen is a good boxer. Another owns a rifle. A third enjoys the allegiance of a tank battalion. Since the means of violence are not possessed by the ruler, it can only exercise control over them so long as those citizens who do possess them are willing to allow it to do so. And they will do this only so long as they perceive this to be in their own interest. Thus, the ruler can only remain the ruler so long as its actions are perceived by a group of citizens who together possess a preponderance of the means of violence existing in the society as being in their own interest to a sufficient degree that it would not be worth their while to replace it with any alternative ruler of which they are aware. The ruler is thus the agent of this group of citizens, hereinafter referred to as a **dominant coalition**, and will remain the ruler only so long as it does their bidding.

Now what is it that the members of a dominant coalition desire? It is economic security. That is, it is a greater assurance that they will be able to satisfy their desires (whatever those desires happen to be) to at least a given degree. Thus, the basic role of the ruler in the economic process is to exercise the power which it controls in such a way as to provide the security desired by a dominant coalition, either by suppressing innovative activity or by causing income and wealth to be transferred directly in accordance with its wishes. It does this in a number of ways.

The following is a list of some of the ways in which the ruler may act to serve the desires of a dominant coalition. The list is by no means complete. The items on the list are quite varied and each could be the subject of a book in itself, but they have one thing in common. They are all examples of the use of coercion in the economic process in behalf of a specific group of individuals—not the same group in every case, but a specific group, nonetheless.

1. Settling disputes over property rights

    Examples: Enforcing contracts
    Settling estates
    Resolving tort actions

2. Undertaking collective consumption and raising the funds necessary to finance it

    Examples: National defense
    Social security
    Highway building

3. Specifying the rights and duties of the parties to a transaction

    Examples: "Truth-in-lending" laws
    "Truth-in-packaging" laws
    Certain securities laws

4. Seizing property for public use, either with or without compensation

    Examples: Nationalization of industry
    Eminent domain
    Military conscription

5. Regulating the economic activity of firms (that is, certain aspects of their prices, outputs, products, profits, promotions, and the like)

    Examples: Public utility regulation
    The sugar quota system
    The National Industrial Recovery Act of 1933

6. Specifying the types of agreements which individuals may enter into

    Examples: Antitrust laws
    Antidiscrimination laws
    Policy toward collective bargaining

7. Restricting the ability of certain buyers and sellers to engage in trade

   Examples: Tariffs
   Price controls
   Licensing

8. Subsidizing certain individuals at the expense of others

   Examples: Welfare
   Subsidization of shipbuilding
   Financing of public education

9. Modifying the provisions of existing contracts between individuals

   Examples: Bankruptcy laws
   War powers
   Debt moratoriums

10. Limiting the manner in which individuals may use their property

    Examples: Zoning laws
    Sunday closing laws
    Restrictions on the use of snowmobiles

11. Raising revenue to finance the actions of the ruler

    Examples: Property tax laws
    Excise tax laws
    Income tax laws

12. Acting to influence the level of aggregate income

    Examples: Deficit spending
    Controlling the money supply
    Widespread price and wage controls

As mentioned earlier, the above is not intended as a comprehensive list of possible activities of the ruler in behalf of a dominant coalition. Nor is this whole section of the book intended as a treatise on political science. Rather, its purpose is to employ a very simplified (perhaps even a simplistic) theory of political activity to call attention to a fact which you ignore at your own economic peril. That is simply that the government plays a major role in the economic process. The point is worth repeating. **The government plays a major role in the economic process and, thus, in determining the value of everything you will ever buy or sell.** No one who desires to get the most from his life can afford to ignore that fact.

The economic process is thus characterized by two major phenomena. One of these we have already discussed in considerable detail. This is the free, voluntary activity of households as they make their budgetary allocations, seeking always to satisfy their desires to as great a degree as possible **within the existing set of laws.** This phenomenon was labelled the "invisible hand." The other major phenomenon at work in the economic process should now be clear as well. This is the voluntary activity of households as they seek to **change the existing set of laws** in ways which enable them to more fully satisfy their desires. This activity amounts, as we have seen, to employing the use of force and violence in the achievement of their ends through the agency of a ruler. This aspect of the economic process we will refer to as the "visible hand." It is a hand, again, because it directs the actions of all households subject to the law, but this time it is visible to all. An individual pays his taxes not because he feels that this would be the best use of his money, but because he fears the consequences imposed by the ruler for not paying them.

The Theory of Value

Having now discussed both the visible and the invisible hands, we are ready to discuss the theory of value that is relevant for the world in which you live. As you will see, it is not radically different from our earlier discussion of price determination. It is different, in fact, in only one respect. It considers the role of government. We will discuss first the consequences of the reality of the visible hand for the value of a specific item, and then we will examine its consequences for the level of aggregate economic activity.

What determines the market value of any specific item, be it product or factor of production? This value is the result of a process of bargaining between those who want to obtain the item and those who are offering it for sale. In our previous discussion of value, we saw that movements in market value were determined by the relative bargaining power of these two groups of traders. We also examined many of the things which determine this bargaining power, namely, the numbers of buyers and sellers, the alternatives to trading which they enjoy, the existing set of preferences, expectations, and technology, and a host of others. There was one set of value-determining factors which we did not discuss, however. This was the set of **rules** surrounding the bargaining process.

Every negotiation takes place within the context of a set of rules. There are rules such as grading standards which specify the nature of the product itself. There are rules which specify what the product can be used for. Zoning ordinances would be examples of these. There are rules such as the Occupational Safety and Health Act of 1970 which affect the method by which the product may be produced. There are rules such as the Consumer Credit Protection Act of 1968 which specify what information the parties must disclose to each other in the course of bargaining. There are rules such as licensing ordinances which specify which individuals are eligible to sell. There are rules such as export embargoes which specify which individuals are eligible to buy. Besides these fairly obvious rules, there are the rules resulting from all of the actions of the ruler noted earlier, any one of which will have some impact on the parties to the negotiation. Each of these rules affects either the number of buyers and sellers in the market or the terms on which they are willing to trade. They thus affect the resulting market value. It is thus the case that the value of anything is determined in part by the legal environment, that is, by the set of rules and regulations. **If any one of these rules changes, market values will change as well.** This is a fact which is often overlooked in actual transactions, and the consequences of such an oversight can be catastrophic. It is the major purpose of this entire section on the visible hand to reduce the likelihood that you will commit such an error.

The existence of force and coercion in the economic process thus has important consequences for anyone trying to forecast what the value of something will be in the future. It also has important consequences for the workings of the economic process as a whole, and perhaps even for the nature of that process in future years. To see why, let us return again to our discussion of the business cycle. This time, however, we will consider the role of government.

The Postwar Business Cycle

Earlier in Part II of this book, we discussed the business cycle, that is, the alternate rising and falling of aggregate economic activity. That discussion was, however, carried out under one fairly restrictive assumption, namely, that there was no visible hand. The cycle we described earlier was, in other words, characteristic of a world in which the ruler took no action whatever to modify the workings of the cycle, letting the level of aggregate income rise and fall as it would. This is not, however, the world in which you live. In your world people desire economic security, and they are willing, through the use of a ruler, to apply force in pursuit of it. Why did we then carry out our earlier discussion under such restrictive assumptions? We did it because unless you understand what the cycles would be like without government intervention, you cannot understand the nature of the ruler's response to them. And unless you understand the nature of that response, you cannot fully understand the real-world cycles themselves. This was the reason for our earlier discussion. Aside from this reason, however, the earlier discussion is useful in its own right to describe cycles in the past, that is, before the Great Depression of the 1930's. Prior to that time, governments took very little action to modify the business cycle, and the real-world cycles followed reasonably well the course of our earlier discussion. It may, in fact, be useful to explain the differences between that world and the world of today as a starting point for our discussion of post World War II business cycles.

The topic which we are now about to discuss is one about which relatively little is known. It is, in fact, one of the most unsettled topics in economics. Yet it is a topic which absolutely must be included in this book if it is to accomplish its purpose of helping you get the most out of life. You should, however, be fully aware that what follows will be my own view of the dynamics of the postwar economic process and not the generally-held view of economists as a group. This does not mean that my view is without support, however. It merely means that there is no such thing as a "generally-held view" in this area, and that you should be aware of that fact. With this caution firmly in mind, let us proceed.

The recession of the 1930's was one of the most important events of the last 100 years. It was a recession unlike any before or since. The annual average unemployment rate, which had only exceeded 10 percent once before in the twentieth century, averaged 17.9 percent between 1930 and 1940, reaching a peak of 24.9 percent in the year 1933.[4] It also lasted longer than previous recessions. Whereas during previous twentieth century recessions it had taken only about two years, on average, for the level of manufacturing production to regain the level of the previous peak, it was not until 1937 that this indicator recovered to the level it had reached in 1929 (and not until 1940 that it went above that level to stay.)[5] The recession was also deep. From 1929 to 1933, GNP

---

[4]U.S. Bureau of the Census, **Historical Statistics of the United States, Colonial Times to 1970, Bicentennial Edition,** Washington, D.C., 1975, p. 135.

[5]Ibid., p. 667.

declined by some 46 percent, prices by some 22 percent, and wages (average hourly earnings of production workers in manufacturing) by some 21 percent.[6] These magnitudes were beyond anything experienced in the lifetimes of most of those who lived at that time.

The Great Depression was not important, however, because of the records which it established in economic distress. It was important because of what it did to the thinking of the dominant coalition in nearly every country in the Western world. Prior to 1929, there had been good times and there had been bad. Boom had followed recession for as long as anyone could remember. But faith in the invisible hand remained strong.

The most prominent economists for the previous 150 years had nearly all argued that recessions were the result of accidental events and the excesses which occurred during booms and that the normal condition of the capitalist economy was one of relatively full employment and prosperity. Only the Marxists had argued that economic crises were an inherent part of capitalism and that they were destined to become worse as time went by. The experience of the 1930's profoundly shook this faith in capitalism. As the recession dragged on, more and more people began to question the ability of the economy to recover. Marxism and other radical points of view gained adherents in all the Western countries. Belief in the practicality of an unregulated economic system all but died during the Great Depression.

Even the economics profession turned away from its earlier position. In 1936, a book was published in England which changed the viewpoint of most economists almost at a single stroke. This book was entitled **The General Theory of Employment, Interest, and Money,** and it was written by John Maynard Keynes of Cambridge University. In it, Keynes argued very persuasively that the earlier view had been wrong, that there was no inherent tendency for the capitalist economy to recover from the recession, and that, if it failed to do so, the only way to regain prosperity was for the ruler to take active measures to bring this about. The economy may regain full employment in the long run, said Mr. Keynes, but, as he put it, " In the long run we are all dead."

The Keynesian solution was relatively simple. If the cause of the recession was the disappearance of investment during the crisis, then the cure would be to offset the positive net savings which occurred (a leakage out of the circular flow) with an "injection " into the flow of government spending in excess of tax receipts. Deficit spending was thus the answer. The ruler should either cut taxes so the households

---

[6]Ibid., pp. 170, 224.

could spend more or it should spend more on its own. The deficit (that is, the excess of government spending over tax receipts) could be financed by government borrowing from the central bank.[7] This borrowing would create enough new money to finance the deficit, and the size of the circular flow would increase.

The anguish, fear, and extreme pessimism of the depression years, together with the persuasiveness of **The General Theory** and the obvious success of the deficits during World War II in restoring full employment, thus wrought a profound change in the thinking of the dominant coalitions in most Western countries, and, specifically for our purposes, in the United States. No more did they believe that the economic process would restore prosperity in short order. No more did they believe that it was wrong for the ruler to try to restore prosperity through "spending beyond its means." No more was the national debt looked upon as something to be minimized at any cost. As a result of this change of attitude, the ruler responded, and in 1946 a law was passed in the United States entitled The Employment Act of 1946. This law made it the legal obligation of the United States government to take whatever measures it felt were needed to maintain a high level of employment and prosperity in the United States. As a result, the character of the business cycle has profoundly changed.

If you were to examine data from a statistical source such as **Historical Statistics of the United States, Colonial Times to 1970,** you would find that before World War II the behavior of the U.S. economy was essentially as described in our earlier discussion. Recessions were characterized by falling aggregate income, a falling money supply, rising unemployment, falling wages, and falling prices. Booms were characterized by the opposite. Since World War II, however, the picture has changed drastically. Aggregate real income (that is, aggregate income corrected for changes in the price level) and unemployment still behave much as they did before. That is, even though the magnitude of the changes is substantially smaller than during the earlier period, income falls during recession and unemployment rises and the opposite occurs during booms. With the other series, however, the story is quite different. Since the early 1950's, there has been very little if any tendency for the level of prices, the level of wages, or the supply of money to follow the cycles in aggregate income and unemployment. Rather, these three series all follow a remarkably smooth path, ignoring the

---

[7]A "central bank" is not a commercial bank but a governmental or quasi-governmental agency which conducts monetary policy (to be discussed later). In the United States, the central bank is called the Federal Reserve System.

cycles almost completely, and increasing secularly at an apparently increasing rate, at least through 1978. Thus, it is no longer true that prices and wage levels fall significantly during recessions. Rather, they seem to ignore the cycle and rise over the long pull. This phenomenon is called **inflation,** and it has become the most significant aspect of the post World War II economic process.

What is inflation? How does it come about? Can we expect it to continue? What will the consequences be if it does continue? These are the questions to which I will provide **my** answers in the pages which follow. Again, let me remind you that this is an area in which a good deal of controversy exists, and you may want to examine other opinions as well.

The first question is easy to answer. Inflation is the name given to a general increase in the price level. An increase in any specific price is not an indication of inflation. Individual prices can be expected to increase for a variety of reasons. They can also be expected to decrease. It is only when the set of prices which are rising are not offset by the set which are falling that the general level of prices, the **price index** if you prefer, is rising and we have inflation.

The second question is almost as easy. Inflation can only occur if either the supply of money is increasing relative to the supply of goods and services or if individuals are spending the money at a faster and faster rate as they receive it. Since there is little to suggest that the latter is a long-term phenomenon, we may conclude that the major cause of inflation is an increase in the supply of money in the circular flow relative to the supply of goods and services.

How does this relative increase in the money supply come about? This is a somewhat more complex issue, but it should not prove overly difficult if we recall our earlier discussion of the business cycle, at the same time bearing in mind the changed attitude of the dominant coalition toward the ruler's role in altering that cycle. Inasmuch as a complete repetition of our earlier discussion would be unnecessarily tedious, we will merely recall those parts which seem necessary.

Recall our earlier discussion of the recession phase of the cycle. Among the major features of this phase were positive net savings as aggregate investment spending fell below aggregate saving and a contraction of the money supply as borrowing decreased. As you recall, these two developments were not the cause of the recession but they did add to the cumulative nature of the contraction. If, as is now the case, the ruler feels an obligation to minimize the severity of the recession, it will do one or both of two things. First, it will act to offset the leakage of net savings out of the circular flow with an injection of government spending which is not offset by tax payments. Second, it will act to increase the free reserves of the commercial banks, thus making them more likely to make additional loans. The first of these constitutes an expansive **fiscal policy**, and the second constitutes an expansive **monetary policy**.

Thus, one new feature of the postwar recession is a strong attempt by the ruler to resist the decrease in aggregate income through deficit spending and an expansive monetary policy. This attempt seems, in fact, to be sufficiently strong that the money supply is kept from falling significantly, and the demand for goods and services remains sufficiently strong that the average levels of prices and wages do not decline significantly either. (A second new feature of the postwar economy, the widespread use of collective bargaining in the labor market, also contributes to the latter result.)

Turning now to the recovery phase, we recall that the prewar recession was ended by an increase in the ratio of consumption spending to aggregate income, a fall in the prices of productive factors, and the recollection that all prior recessions had come to an end. In the postwar cycle, the situation is different. Factor prices do not fall significantly during the postwar recession. Hence, if the entrepreneur is to be induced to innovate again it will be less by a drop in the expected cost of his project than by an increase in the returns he expects to obtain from doing so. Rather than the investment climate becoming favorable through falling costs, in other words, it becomes favorable through rising expected receipts. This is, of course, something of an over-simplification. One cost should decline faster during the postwar recession, and this is the cost of capital. As a result of the expansionary monetary policy, the commercial banks will have more free reserves at any given point in the recession than they would otherwise have had and should, therefore, be willing to make any given loan at a lower rate of interest. This will cause some decline in the cost of innovation. This decline will not be as great as the prewar decline, however, so much of the recovery in innovation will still be based upon the rise in expected returns. This rise is caused, of course, by the apparent end of the recession while product prices remain at relatively high levels, and this is due, in turn, to the easing of pessimism resulting from the expansive policies of the ruler.

Another feature of the recovery is also now present which was absent before the war. This is the continuation of the expansionary policies of the ruler. As has been said so often in this book, the future is uncertain. And it is no less uncertain for the ruler than it is for anyone else. Thus, rather than risking a resumption of the recession, the ruler will extend the expansionary policies until it becomes quite clear that the recovery has come to stay.

Now consider the boom. During the boom everything is going fine.

Unemployment is decreasing, aggregate income is increasing, everyone is happy. This, of course, makes the ruler happy and makes it reluctant to do anything to upset things. One of the things which Keynes had said ought to be done during the boom was that a sort of negative deficit spending ought to take place. That is, taxes ought to exceed government spending. Another is that the level of free reserves in the banking system should be held down in order to prevent an undue rise in the number of loans. Both of these things are unpopular. Both will dampen the boom and might (since the future is uncertain) even bring about the crisis. Hence, there is a strong tendency among rulers to apply the Keynesian contractionary prescription in a half-hearted manner. The surplus budgets of the boom don't quite offset the previous deficits, and the reductions in free reserves never quite offset the previous increases. Thus, while prices don't decline much in the postwar recessions, they do rise during the booms. And so do factor prices.

Finally, let's consider the crisis. As the boom progresses, the ratio of savings over income gradually rises, thus causing a reduction in the rate of growth of the circular flow. At the same time, the prices of productive factors continue to rise. These two developments, plus the recollection of past crises, cause the optimism of the boom to fade, and at length the crisis occurs. Innovation declines, sales and employment begin to decline, and the money supply stops growing and begins to contract. Now the course of the ruler is clear. Now to delay too long is dangerous. Hence, the ruler moves quickly and decisively toward an expansionary monetary policy and a deficit budget, and we move into another postwar recession.

This, then, is the postwar business cycle as it appears to me. It is the result of both the visible and the invisible hand, of both voluntary and involuntary action. It is the environment in which you live, and its basic features should be well understood. These are, as we have seen, increases and declines in aggregate income, increases and decreases in unemployment, innovation during recovery and boom and creative destruction during recession, but a money supply which grows more during booms than it falls during recessions, and, thus, price and wage levels which do the same.

When one takes a longer-term view, one encompassing a number of cycles, the level of prices, the level of wages, and the supply of money are seen to rise. This is the inflation which we mentioned earlier. It is caused by the supply of money outrunning the supply of goods and services. The money supply increases during the boom as borrowing takes place from the increased level of free reserves created by the ruler during the recession, and does not decrease during the recession as the ruler fights to restore prosperity. Since the money supply increases over time, prices will rise unless the real output of goods and services can increase fast enough to offset this through the process of economic development. This has apparently not happened in the postwar world.

Another phenomenon is also apparent when one takes the long-term view, a phenomenon about which we will have more to say in Part III. This is the tendency for the inflation to accelerate, that is, for the rate of price increase to itself increase through time at an increasing rate. To understand the reason for this tendency, let us recall again the reason for the inflation in the first place.

The inflation is caused by the asymmetric manner in which the ruler acts to smooth out the business cycle, moving much more decisively to moderate the recession than to moderate the boom. It does this because the dominant coalition has a much greater dislike of unemployment than it has of the levels of inflation which it has experienced thus far. Thus, the basic objective of the ruler is to hold the level of unemployment at a level which is satisfactorily low from the viewpoint of the dominant coalition, and this level is below that which would prevail in the absence of government intervention.

Now unemployment, that is, an excess of the quantity of labor skills supplied over the quantity demanded, is, as we saw from our earlier discussion, nothing more than an indication that the price of labor, the wage, is too high to bring the supply of labor into equality with the demand. Now it is the **relative price** of labor that is too high. As we saw earlier, prices only have meaning in relationship to other prices. If all prices were doubled (along with the dollar values of all assets) very little would be changed. But if the price of item A rises while the price of item B remains the same, you will have all of the revising of budgets, changes in demands, and so forth, which we have already considered as households adjust to the new situation. Thus, what is needed to correct unemployment is a decline in the relative price of labor. This will eventually occur by itself as the recession runs its course, that is, as the sellers of labor skills become reconciled to the lack of demand for their services and offer to work for less. If the ruler is unwilling (or unable) to accept this solution, however, he must decrease the relative price of labor by raising the expected price of everything except labor in the mind of the entrepreneur. This is the basic reason why the expansive policies of the ruler reduce unemployment in the recession. It will only work, however, so long as workers do not also come to expect the relative increase in the prices of other things. If they do so, that is, if they come to expect this increase, they will also recognize the decrease in the relative wage rate that they are being asked to accept, and whatever caused the wage to be too high to prevent unemployment in the first place will do so again. Hence, the only way by which the ruler can reduce unemployment is by "fooling" the workers into accepting a lower relative wage rate than they believe they are getting. Obviously, this cannot work in the long run. Once the workers recognize what has happened, they will ask the same relative wage rate as before, and the unemployment will return. If, however, the ruler is compelled to maintain the low rates of unemployment desired by the dominant coalition, it has one option left. It can "fool" the workers again by raising other prices once more. This will only work, of course, until they begin to expect repeated price increases, that is, until they come to expect continuing inflation. Once this occurs, the only course open to the ruler that is compelled to maintain low rates of unemployment is to fool them again by increasing prices by more than they expected it to. And once they come to expect the greater price increases, it must resort to even greater ones. In other words, if the ruler must maintain a level of unemployment below that which would have occurred without its intervention, the result will be a secularly accelerating inflation much like that which we see around us today. Whether this situation will continue or not, and what we might expect if it does continue, are matters which we will discuss in Part III.

So ends our discussion of the business cycle in the postwar world, and with it our discussion of the theory of value. If you will go back from time to time and study well the contents of Part II, you will gain an understanding of the economic process which I honestly feel is **much more** than equivalent to what you would have gotten in any college course in economics of which I have ever heard prior to writing this book. Furthermore, it will be an understanding which will be **useful** to you in your efforts to get the most out of life. If you will make the effort to understand this material well, it will be one of the best allocations of time you ever made.

Now, let us turn to the finale—the drawing together and summing up of the major lessons to be learned from Parts I and II—the wisdom of economics.

Part III

The Wisdom of Economics

Not long ago, my wife and I attended a banquet. As we chatted with the couple seated across the table from us, it became known that I taught economics. At that point, the response of our companions went somewhat as follows. "Economics! Oh my, that is a hard subject. I had an economics course back in college, but I just barely got through it. All those graphs and formulas....I'm glad somebody understands that stuff."

Unfortunately, this was not an isolated incident. Economics is one of the most misunderstood of subjects. Many think of it as nothing but ivory-tower theorizing. Others view it as something that economists and politicians ought to be concerned about, but not themselves. Many just consider it incomprehensible. Most have only the vaguest idea as to what it even is.

Now this would be understandable if one were talking about nuclear physics or radio astronomy. These subjects are, in fact, the realm of the specialist. Economics, however, is not. Economics is intensely practical. It is profoundly relevant for every single human being who ever lived. It is relevant because it can be applied by each of them in their own individual lives. Furthermore, it has some profound implications.

It is the purpose of Part III to present some of these implications. What follows is the most important part of this book. It is essentially a statement of what I consider to be the most profound lessons which can be obtained from the study of economics **insofar as the individual human being is concerned.** They are not lessons for the statesman. They are not lessons for those who formulate monetary policy, who regulate railroads, or who legislate taxes. They are lessons for **you** as you make your way in life. Many of the lessons will not appear surprising. Many will appear to be "plain common sense." But they are more than that. They are straightforward implications of the economic principles presented in this book. By and large, they could be taken to constitute a body of good advice, the kind which you might expect from a wise old grandfather, for example. And yet they are more than the advice of experience. They will agree with such advice, but they are something more. What I am trying to say is that there is a **better reason** for taking these lessons to heart than that you were taught them by a wise and respected grandfather, a worldly uncle who had made a fortune, or someone who has been through the "school of hard knocks." These lessons have a logical basis. They are based on solid reasoning. They are not a single man's opinion, no matter how wise he may be, but the implications of centuries of accumulated analysis by hundreds of the wisest individuals who have ever considered these matters. Consequently, you ought to consider them very carefully and reject them only if you yourself can prove them wrong. It was in the hope of providing credibility to some excellent advice that Part III of this book was written.

With this then as an introduction, let us turn to the lessons of economics.

Lesson 1: You have an economic problem, and you will solve it

Your economic problem is this. You will not be able to satisfy all your desires. Consequently, you must decide which of those desires are going to be satisfied and which are not. You can either make this decision in a conscious, systematic manner such as that explained in Part I or you can let the rush of events solve your problem for you. You can, in other words, either be at the helm of your ship or you can let the wind and the currents decide your course. The attempt to solve your problem consciously, while bothersome, time-consuming, and in no sense precise, will, nonetheless, give you an understanding as to the nature of that problem which can be gained in no other way. It is my belief that it will also lead to a much better solution from your point of view.

Lesson 2: Everyone has an economic problem

Part I of this book was, as you recall, a fairly detailed account as to how a person might proceed in order to consciously solve his economic problem. Part I of this book was written to everyone. As was stated in the very first paragraph, **everyone** has an economic problem. No one can do all they would like to do. All of us have desires which will never be fulfilled. We all experience frustration.

You might think about this the next time you start feeling sorry for yourself.

Lesson 3: A conscious solution to your economic problem will give a sense of purpose to your life

Recall for a moment our discussion in Part I. What was the very first step in the conscious solution to your economic problem? It was to decide what you wanted to do with the rest of your life. If you don't know this, there is no way for you to attain a goal that you view as really worthwhile. Your life will seem meaningless and purposeless—as, indeed, it will be. Once you have made this decision, however, the question of a purpose in life is solved. All that remains is to decide how to use your assets so as to best attain this purpose. And what this actually amounts to is ordering your life in such a way that every single action you take, from going to bed early to attending night school, is a purposeful, meaningful act in that it contributes toward the attainment of your lifetime goal. Selecting a lifetime goal is thus an absolute prerequisite to an optimal solution to your economic problem. In plain English, this means that there is nothing you can do in this life that will yield you more satisfaction, more sense of purpose, and more sense of accomplishment than selecting a philosophy of life, a religion if you will, which you are really willing to base your life upon. The search for such a religion should be your most important task.

Lesson 4: A conscious solution to your economic problem will make your assets seem more adequate

A conscious solution to your economic problem will free you to a considerable extent from social pressures to which you would otherwise be more sensitive. Once you have gone through a process such as that explained in Part I, you will know **why** you are doing the things you are doing, why, for example, you drive a certain type of car, why you don't belong to a certain club. You will be doing them because they are the best way you know of to accomplish **your** goals in life. You will realize that since other people's actions are based upon their goals, and since there is no reason to expect their goals to coincide with your goals, there is no reason to suppose that you ought to be doing what others are doing. You will be able to justify your actions to yourself, in other words, in a way that will make you less susceptible to fads, fashions, and social pressures to do certain things than you otherwise would be. Unless you have really thought through the solution to your economic problem, you will constantly be trying to imitate the budgetary decisions of others. You will be trying to "keep up with the Jones," so to speak. Furthermore, since you will also be trying to keep up with the Smiths and the Browns, you will be trying to match each of them **in those areas where they place their greatest emphasis**. Consequently, your assets will appear much less adequate to you than if you realized that the Jones are doing their thing and that you should be doing your thing and not trying to do theirs as well. Consequently, a conscious solution to your economic problem should increase your satisfaction even if you were to wind up doing exactly as you would have done without going through the allocative process.

Lesson 5: The cost of any course of action consists of what you must sacrifice in order to pursue it

Everything you do in life has a cost, and that cost is always the same. It is what you must forego in order to pursue the course of action you select. We saw in Part I that we are all subject to the constraints imposed on us by our assets. We saw that the solution to our economic problem implies the allocation of all of these assets to whichever particular purpose we select. There is no slack. You cannot add new things to your list of satisfied desires without removing others to make room for them. No matter how you look at it, your assets are fixed. Even if you were to receive a windfall gain that was totally unexpected, your assets would still be fixed. They would be greater in size, but they would be fixed.

The way to determine the cost of anything is crystal clear. This cost is not the amount of time or money which is required to enjoy it. It is the other enjoyments which you must sacrifice in order to free up this time and money. Assume, for example, that you are considering the purchase of another car. How will you pay for it? Since your assets are fixed, the only way in which you can do this is by not paying for something else, that is, by going without some other desirable experiences which you could have enjoyed had you not chosen to purchase the car. Precisely what those foregone experiences will be is, of course, up to you to decide. This does not concern us here. Our point is simply that **there will be something foregone**. The relevance of this point to you is that you should try to identify what this sacrifice will be. Only by doing so can you correctly decide whether the car is worth the cost.

Lesson 6: Don't compare your accomplishments with the accomplishments of others

You are unique. There is no one else like you. There never was such a person, and there never will be. You are one of a kind.

Your uniqueness is defined by your set of assets. This set is unique. No one else in this entire world has the same set of assets as you have. Consequently, no one else in this entire world should be expected to enjoy the same set of satisfactions that you enjoy. No two people, in other words, are likely to select identical solutions to their economic problems. This being the case, it is a serious mistake to judge your own performance in life by the performance of others. You might envy others if you choose because you judge their assets to be superior to your own, but don't judge your performance on the basis of the results that they achieve. Never condemn your own performance because another person attained an objective which you could not. It is not your task in life to beat others. Your task is to make the most of the set of assets which **you** possess. Your performance can only be judged in relation to your potential. Study the actions of others for clues as to how you might improve your own performance. Imitate whatever useful techniques that you see them employ. But don't judge your performance by their results. To do so is to base your judgement upon an incorrect view of the world. Drive yourself just as hard as you choose. Set your goal as high as you want. But don't judge your success by the performance of others. They are not running in the same race as you. They did not start the game with your set of chips.

Lesson 7: There is always an element of luck

Every decision which you will ever make will be made in the context of uncertainty. This is absolutely unavoidable, and it is unavoidable for a very simple reason. The consequences of any decision occur in the future, and the future is uncertain. This uncertainty can be reduced, of course, by gathering more information, but this can only be done at a cost. First, there is the very real possibility that while you are gathering additional information someone else will seize the opportunity which you are considering. Second, the gathering of information requires time and money which could be spent in other ways. The only thing about which there is no uncertainty is the past. And no one can take advantage of past opportunities.

Since uncertainty will always be present at the making of decisions, every decision must be made in the absence of some pieces of information which are critical to its outcome. Every decision must be made, in other words, on the basis of certain assumptions. If these assumptions turn out to be correct, all well and good. But they may not. An assumption is essentially a guess. It may be an informed guess. It may be based upon years of experience. But it remains a guess. And any guess can turn out to be wrong. Furthermore, it can turn out to be wrong **through no fault of the decision-maker**. For the reasons noted above, it will always be proper procedure to make your decisions in the absence of complete information. You should, of course, obtain all the information which you feel is necessary, but you can never obtain it all. And whenever you lack information, you must make assumptions. This being the case, it is entirely possible for someone to make a decision correctly (that is, using the correct decision-making process) and still have an unfortunate outcome. If an individual were to make a long series of decisions, then, presumably, superior wisdom and insight would result in a high proportion of favorable outcomes. It does not follow, however, that if you fall far short of your (reasonable) goal you have lived your life poorly or that if you exceed your expectations you have demonstrated superior intelligence. People do make a great many decisions, and the wisdom and intelligence of the decision-makers do have an impact on the percent of these which turn out favorably. But not all decisions are of equal importance. Most people make only a few very large decisions in life, and when the game is only played a few times, anything is possible. For this reason, you should not be too hard on yourself if a venture turns out badly, and you shouldn't be too proud if one turns out well. It was not altogether your fault in either case. What is important in judging your performance is how you make your decisions, not how any one of them comes out. And this is indicated by the results of all of your decisions, not by the results of any small group of them.

Lesson 8: Knowledge is power

In a world of uncertainty, knowledge is power. It will enable its possessor to act while those without it remain paralyzed by uncertainty. If both act at the same time, it will improve its possessor's decisions. Consequently, few things are as crucial to your success in attaining your goals in life as access to information—information which is accurate and which is also current enough to be useful.

Lesson 9: Never cease to think of yourself as an entrepreneur

The very essence of economic life is change. Innovation is always taking place. As a result, all established market positions are continually being worn away. Some positions are worn away more slowly, of course, but all are worn away. The implication of this is very simple: you cannot rest on your laurels.

The economic process is risky. It offers no sheltered havens. You should never cease to view it as risky. You should never cease to recognize the very real possibility that the specialty in which you are currently engaged will become much less rewarding than it has been in the past. You should never cease looking for alternative courses of action which you might pursue should this, in fact, occur. Thus, you should never cease viewing yourself as an entrepreneur. If you do, you are living in a dream world, and, by so doing, you are courting disaster.

Failure to learn this lesson is, I suspect, very common. I also suspect that it results in untold hardship and disappointment. The process goes something like this. An individual innovates. He goes into business, for example, or he acquires a skill. At the time he does this he has other options, he examines each of these options, and he makes his choice. He is quite aware at this point that he is taking a risk. Then time passes. More and more, his time and efforts are absorbed in his attempt to succeed at the course he has chosen. Less and less does he pay attention to matters beyond his immediate sphere of concern. Gradually, he comes to see himself and his efforts in a different light. His perception of himself changes from that of an entrepreneur to that of an innkeeper. It changes from that of an entrepreneur to that of an engineer. He becomes unable to distinguish clearly between himself and his chosen specialty. He is in trouble.

He is in trouble because of the nature of the process in which he is engaged. No one can expect to continue in the same specialty for the rest of his life. Competition will not permit it. Consequently, when he ceases to view himself as an entrepreneur who is currently engaged in the provision of engineering skills or as an entrepreneur who is currently in the innkeeping business and begins, instead, to view himself as an engineer or as an innkeeper, he has virtually assured his destruction. He has assured that he will go down with his ship. Specialties are doomed by the economic process. Individuals are not. Specialties should be viewed as vehicles which are to be driven as far as they will go and then replaced with another. Nobody goes to the junk yard with their old car, but many go to the junk yard with their old specialty. They do this because it is harder to change specialties than it is to change cars. And it is even harder to change specialties if one has stopped searching for specialties to change to, that is, if one has ceased viewing either himself or herself as an entrepreneur.

Life is a series of ventures, and as soon as one venture is undertaken, you should be looking forward to the next. Only in this way can you cope with the changing conditions inherent in the economic process.

Lesson 10: There is no such thing as intrinsic value

Nothing has a constant value in and of itself. The value of anything is determined by the degree to which it will satisfy the desires of people, and this will vary according to time and circumstance. Whether you are considering a share of common stock, an automobile, or a glass of water, their values will all fluctuate, and they will all be determined by the factors explained in Part II, namely, the relative bargaining power of those who desire to obtain the items and those who desire to provide them and all the factors upon which those, in turn, depend.

Lesson 11: You must look beyond the present

In part II of this book, it was stated that in order to satisfy as many of your desires as possible you must engage in a never-ending process of changing the composition of the set of assets which you possess. That is, you must be continually removing assets and replacing them with other assets in such a way as to increase the value of the set of assets itself. Now the value of this set of assets, and of any single asset within it, is dependent upon the degree to which it will enable you to satisfy your own desires or the desires of other people in the future. Consequently, you must orient your thinking toward the future. You must examine market forces as they exist at present, analyze those forces, and from them predict how desirable the services of the various assets will be in the future. Furthermore, you must do this more accurately than people in general. This is because other individuals would also like to hold those assets which will be more useful in the future. Consequently, you must identify assets which will be more useful in the future than other people expect them to be. Only if you do this will they be willing to make the asset exchanges which you desire. Thus, you must predict the future usefulness of assets more accurately than others, and this can only be done if your thoughts are directed not at current developments, but at what those developments imply for the future. You must, in short, look as far ahead as possible.

Lesson 12: Good opportunities will never seek you out

As should be obvious from our discussion thus far, the economic process is very complex. A great many factors affect the value of any single item, so many, in fact, that one can only really investigate a limited number of opportunities. This being the case, the theory of value presented in Part II is probably much more useful in evaluating those opportunities that come to your attention than it is in discovering opportunities in the first place. This is, of course, very important, as the ability to recognize a good opportunity when you see it is of tremendous value, but the question naturally arises as to how you learn about opportunities to begin with. The following suggestions are implied from our discussion in Part II.

First of all, you should do everything you can to keep in touch with economic developments in your locality. Read the business page of your local newspaper. Join clubs to which business people belong. Try to become acquainted with as many entrepreneurs as you possibly can. Do things, in other words, which will place you in conversations in which opportunities are likely to be discussed.

Second, and of perhaps even greater importance, recall our discussion in Part II of this book, specifically where we discussed the search for a specialty within the division of labor. Do you recall how it was stated there that the way to induce others to satisfy your desires is to satisfy theirs? The implication of this is that there is probably no better way to discern genuine opportunity than to approach the task with the following questions foremost in your thoughts. How can I be of service? What do people in this area need? How can I give it to them? What needs to be done here? If you can provide a genuine service to people, they will gladly pay you for it. In fact, they will welcome you with open arms. Your only problem will then be determining how to provide that service at a cost which is low enough to yield a profit. Think of others, therefore, and how you can help them solve their economic problems. If you succeed, they might just increase your assets dramatically.

The third implication of our previous discussion is the clearest of all. In fact, it is virtually certain. It is that the truly good opportunities will **not** be thrust upon you. They will not appear in magazine ads. They will not be sent through the mail. Good opportunities are vigorously sought out and, when found, are carefully guarded. Good opportunities do not **have** to seek investors, and you should be very, **very** skeptical of any opportunity that does so. The same thing goes for any formula, scheme, or secret that is alleged to produce wealth. The reason here is that all such schemes, even if they were successful at first, quickly self-destruct when a large number of people attempt to employ them at once. General investment principles do not, of course, have this characteristic, but the more specific the instructions are, the more skeptical you should be. Once any such scheme becomes common knowledge, it becomes worthless.

Lesson 13: Don't take the legal environment for granted

As was pointed out in Part II, the values of all assets, all products, and all factors of production are intimately related to the "rules of the game," that is, to the set of laws existing at the time. Any change in this set of laws will have an impact on all market values.

These laws, as we have seen, are not dictated from on high. They reflect little more than the desires of a dominant coalition, and they are subject to change at any time. Consequently, you should never take the laws as given. Always consider the possibility that they will change and the impact which likely changes might have on the outcome of your decisions. More than one person has purchased a home on the assumption of a particular set of zoning laws only to be sadly disappointed when they were changed. Beyond merely trying to predict changes in the law, you should also be aware of your ability to influence those changes. If you can muster sufficient support, you can have an impact on the legal environment. You can obtain rule changes which will further your interests, and you can prevent changes which will hurt you. This is not easy to do, but you should be aware of the possibility. In any case, you should never forget that every decision involves an assumption about the legal environment which will prevail, and you should do all that is reasonable to assure yourself that this assumption is justified.

Lesson 14: Don't ignore the business cycle

The economic process is cyclical in nature. As we saw in Part II, aggregate income depends primarily upon the level of innovation, and the level of innovation is determined by the alternating waves of optimism and pessimism which run through the economic system. The cycles are inherent in the system. They will be present as long as the free market exists. The relevance of this to you is quite clear. You should expect them to continue—but, as explained in Part II, to continue in a modified form. Expect a crisis at the end of every boom and a recovery at the end of every recession. Make a serious effort to remain informed about the stage of the cycle in which you are operating. Don't make any investment which can only succeed in perpetual boom. Look for assets which are temporarily undervalued in a recession but which will recover when optimism returns. Only by doing this can you do well in the economic process. Those who ignore the cycles, who believe the prophecies of either eternal prosperity or of absolute collapse, stand a very strong chance of being **systematically** ruined by the economic process. They will not only miss the opportunities which exist at the end of the recession, but they will be blind to the danger which exists in the boom (and which grows greater and greater as the boom proceeds). The economic process is not kind to such people. Don't become one of them.

Expect the recessions. Don't overextend yourself during booms. Live within your means as you view those means over the entire cycle. Maintain an asset reserve to help you through hard times. The economic process is a heartless thing. Indeed, it can be absolutely brutal. I believe, however, that much of the hardship that is often attributed to it is really the fault of the individuals themselves. Specifically, to their failure to understand it as it is. There is a strong tendency, I believe, for people to forget the cycle. Like the grasshopper in the fairy tale, they behave as if the boom will go on forever, as if it were the normal state of affairs. And they allocate their resources accordingly. Then, when the recession comes and it becomes apparent that they've been living in a dream world, they suffer losses and deprivation which they could have readily avoided had they been more aware of the nature of the process. In saying this, I don't mean to imply that you should become obsessed with preparing for the next recession. Governments today have a number of programs designed to ease the recessionary pain, and it is to be hoped that such things as unemployment insurance, deposit insurance, and debt moratoriums will be there if needed. Just be aware of the nature of the cycle, and bear in mind the fact that these government programs, like all other aspects of the legal environment, are subject to change if circumstances dictate.

Thus, you should expect the cycles to continue. One thing which you should **not** expect, however, is that prices and wages will fall appreciably during recessions. For reasons explained in Part II, falling prices and wages have not been characteristic of U.S. recessions since 1950. Some have fallen, of course, but, when considered as a group, prices and wages have not fallen appreciably. Whether they would do so if a really major recession came along is anyone's guess, of course, but I am inclined to doubt it. I could be wrong.

Lesson 15: You probably ought to expect secular inflation for a long time to come

The first thing you should note about this lesson is the word "probably." The reason for this is that I simply do not know what the future holds in this regard. Still, a few thoughts are suggested by our previous discussion, and, since you will each have to face this issue for yourselves, I feel that I ought to present them for your consideration. Please keep in mind that there are **no** real authorities in this area, and take these thoughts for what they might be worth.

As explained in Part II, the major difference between the old-style business cycle and the cycles which have existed since 1950 seems to be the attitude of government. Specifically, since the Great Depression, the U.S. government has been much more prone to take measures to lengthen booms and to counteract recessions than it ever was before. The result of this change in attitude has been that the ruler imposes an asymmetry on the cycle by making a more determined effort to moderate recessions than it makes to moderate booms. By so doing, it increases the bargaining power of the sellers of both products and factors of production vis-a-vis the buyers. Because of this, sellers are able to prevail to a greater extent than was previously the case, and prices rise during the boom, do not fall during the recession, and rise secularly from cycle to cycle.

So long as it is the intent of the ruler to hold the rate of unemployment below what it would have been in the absence of his intervention, the rate of inflation must accelerate through time. The reason for this phenomenon was explained in Part II and will not be repeated here. Whether or not this has been happening in the United States is open to debate, of course, but I am inclined toward the position that it has. If this is indeed the case, where will it all end? Are we heading, as some suggest, for another great depression? Are we heading for the imposition of permanent wage and price controls? What **is** likely to happen?

Perhaps we should note first of all that the change in the attitude of government has not stopped the process of creative destruction. The least-desired products are still driven from the market during recessions, the only difference being that this now occurs in the context of stable-price or rising-price recessions rather than falling-price recessions. Consequently, there is probably no significant tendency for abnormally large segments of the productive structure to get out of adjustment with the existing pattern of consumer demand. Many writers on this subject seem to believe that there is such a tendency, but I feel that they confuse cyclical movements with the secular trend. It is true that such segments will develop during booms which are made abnormally long via government stimulation, but such malallocation should be largely corrected during the periods of creative destruction which follow. (At least I feel that this has probably been the case so far in the United States.) What we are considering here is something quite different, namely, the behavior of the system secularly, that is, over a number of cycles. And it is probably not true that there has been a secular growth in the degree to which the productive structure of the economy fails to reflect the pattern of consumer demand.

There may very well be another problem, however. This concerns the nature of the demand pattern itself. As an inflation continues, people come to expect it. When this occurs, they begin to solve their economic problems, to formulate their budgets, with the expectation that inflation will continue. This will almost certainly result in a change in the final allocation of their assets which they select as optimal. That is to say, when people base their allocative decisions on the expectation of inflation, their relative demands for certain items become greater than they would have been had stable prices been expected. Thus, the pattern of demand itself becomes distorted in an inflationary environment. This means that the pattern of demand to which production adjusts itself during an inflation is not the same pattern to which it adjusts when prices are stable.

Why is this important? It is important because if this distortion in the pattern of consumer demand has occurred, then it will be somewhat painful for us to abandon the inflationary course which we are following. To abandon such a course would "undistort" the pattern of relative demands, would reveal a significant discrepancy between the productive structure (geared as it would be to serving the inflationary demand pattern) and the "undistorted" pattern of demand, and would require a period of creative destruction to eliminate this discrepancy.

Yet it is clear that we **will** abandon the course we are following. Accelerating inflation is simply not a viable alternative for the long run. The only question is how it will be abandoned. If the abandonment takes the form of permanently adopting whatever rate of inflation the consumers expect at the time of abandonment, then the expectations of consumers need not change (unless, of course, they had expected acceleration) and the readjustment will be relatively mild, amounting in fact to a restoration of the cycles in unemployment and aggregate real income which would have prevailed had the ruler never intervened to begin with. This form of abandonment is only possible, of course, until the expected rate of inflation has risen above the highest level which the dominant coalition finds acceptable over the long run. Once this point is passed, then the only option remaining is to move to a constant rate of inflation below the rate expected at the time of abandonment. If so, then the greater the difference between the rate that consumers anticipate and the maximum rate which can be accepted on a permanent basis, the greater the readjustment of relative demands, and the more severe the creative destruction will be.

What **will** occur?

My guess would be something like the following.

What matters most in the future will be, of course, the desires of the dominant coalition. Whatever policies they want will ultimately carry the day. What will they want? My guess is that they will want a continuation of the present course, namely, an effort to come as close to eternal prosperity as possible. Thus, I expect the secular rate of inflation to continue to accelerate until it reaches levels sufficiently high to cause them to conclude that their objective is not attainable in the context of a private-enterprise, capitalist economy. (Note that I said I expect the **secular** rate of inflation to accelerate. The annual rates will vary widely as the economy moves through recurrent cycles. It is the long-term trend which concerns us here.) This rate will likely be too high to accept on a permanent basis. At that point, we will either abandon the attempt to moderate recessions, thus leading to a readjustment period of creative destruction of uncertain severity followed by a constant (that is, a non-accelerating) secular inflation at the highest rate which the dominant coalition will accept on a permanent basis, or else we will, in essence, abandon the private-enterprise economy.

The first of these alternatives would mean a readjustment recession during which the change in household expectations would have its effect on the structure of production followed by a series of normal cycles in employment, aggregate income, the money supply, prices, and wages (the last four of these reflecting, of course, the secular rate of inflation adopted). After a long period (probably a decade or more), memories would fade, and we would try once again to eliminate recessions. This would, of course, cause inflation to accelerate again. How this next acceleration would end is anybody's guess, but mine would be that the probability of adopting the second alternative would be greater then than it is now.

The adoption of the second alternative would mean the establishment of some form of widespread wage and price control together with some set of tax changes, subsidies, and other changes in the law which would, in essence, create a centrally-controlled economy. The visible hand would, in other words, become much more important, relative to the invisible hand, than it is today, and the allocation of resources would become largely a matter of politics. If this situation became permanent, the result would very likely be a totalitarian society. If the controls were subsequently relaxed, then we could expect either the resumption of accelerating inflation, an outcome somewhat like alternative one, or a return to controls at a later date. In any event, inflation would be likely to continue in one form or another.

In my view, the only thing which is likely to permanently eliminate inflation is a major shift in the view of the dominant coalition in favor of price stability, even at the cost of higher unemployment. It could well be that such a shift will not take place until an actual majority of the voting population sees itself as being worse off with inflation than it would be with the type of business cycles which occurred during the half century prior to World War II. And as Part II suggests, this could be a good long time.

Lesson 16: If you live in a controlled economy, make every effort to be in control

As this book is being written in the spring of 1979, there exists a very real possibility that the relatively unhampered, free-market economy which we have long enjoyed in the United States may be coming to an end, being replaced with a regime of much greater government control over economic affairs. A number of reasons can be cited in support of this conjecture, among which would be the energy crisis, the environmental crisis, the rising militancy of consumer interests, and the difficulties discussed earlier in attaining low levels of unemployment in the context of stable prices. If such an increase in government control takes place, your course of action must change accordingly.

In order to understand the changes that would be required by this development, recall our earlier discussion of the economic process. In that discussion it was pointed out that one's ability to satisfy his desires was determined by the value of the assets he controlled, and that this value was determined in the marketplace through the interplay of those factors determining the quantities of various items which individuals desire to buy and to sell. The way to prosper in such an enviroment was seen to be through reading the changes in those factors more accurately than the next person. Political factors, while very important in their effect on values, were only one of a great many factors to consider, and the individual would normally expend very little of his assets in political activity. If the role of the ruler in economic affairs increases, however, all this will change. This change will occur for a simple and compelling reason. If the ruler is deciding what is produced, how it is produced, and who gets to consume it, if the ruler is deciding, in other words, who will live in Alaska, who will have the nicest housing, who will vacation in Florida, who will fight fires on a subzero night, and whose children will go to college, then it becomes very important to control the ruler. Political activity will, therefore, have a much higher rate of return than it does at present, and the politicization of everyone can be expected to increase. In such an environment, it is very important that your views be conveyed to those in political office and that those views be supported by as large a coalition as possible.

The politicized economy is a very different thing from the private-enterprise market economy. In the latter, each individual is relatively powerless to change his own environment. He must, therefore, adjust himself to it as best he can, and the best way to do this is, as we have seen, to satisfy the desires of other people. Consequently, when viewed as a whole, the system is essentially one of harmony and cooperation. Frustrations and disappointments exist on the level of the individual decision-maker, of course, but, when viewed as a whole, the system is essentially characterized by harmony. It is generally in your interest to satisfy my desires and in my interest to satisfy yours. In the politicized economy, on the other hand, the environment is basically one of conflict. Here individuals are not forced to resign themselves and make the best of their powerless situations. Instead, they become organized into coalitions, the purpose of each of which is to pursue the interests of its members at the expense of others. Rather than accepting, for the most part, the laws as they are and engaging in voluntary exchange within the context of those laws, individuals, acting as groups, are in a position to change the laws in ways favorable to themselves (to attain, in other words, their ends through the involuntary subjection of others to their wills), and each attempts to do so. The result of this consolidation of powerless individuals into powerful groups is chaotic interruption of the productive process as various groups strike or demonstrate to achieve one objective or another, a clear demonstration of how vulnerable to such tactics we have all become through the division of labor, and in the end, I'm afraid, authoritarian rule by whichever grand coalition becomes powerful enough to impose it.

Now then, what is the relevance of all of this to you? It is simply this. Since those in the dominant coalition can always be expected to pursue their own interests at the expense of others, and since, in a controlled economy, this can make a great deal of difference in the way you live, if the United States should actually move in the direction suggested above, it will become very important for you to be part of the dominant coalition. The earlier you recognize this fact, the better off you will be.

Lesson 17: No one out there is giving away money

This is not a book on investing. That subject is far too complex and far too extensive to be treated in a book such as this. There is one point, however, which I feel is appropriate here as it is a direct implication of our earlier discussion. That is that if anyone ever offers you a deal that is "too good to be true," it isn't. This is the case for a very simple reason. No one ever needs to offer such a deal. Anyone wanting to raise capital can obtain it from an incredible number of sources. Furthermore, he can obtain it at a very reasonable cost, **if he really has a sound project in mind.** Consequently, no one will ever offer you spectacular returns on any investment whatever unless that investment has already proven to be too risky for him to obtain capital at lower cost elsewhere. As a supplier of capital you are in direct competition with literally millions of other individuals, and there is **absolutely no reason whatsoever** to believe that you can obtain more than an average rate of return without also assuming the greater degree of risk that goes with it.

Lesson 18: Things are never either as good or as bad as they seem

The economic process is fraught with illusions. These illusions are created by the process itself. They arise from the failure of individuals to look far enough ahead.

The one thing that you can always bet on in economic life is that everyone is looking for a good thing. Consequently, whenever anyone has a good thing, everyone else is trying to take it away from them. And sooner or later they will succeed. In the long run, the rewards in all industries tend toward equality. The rewards in all professions do the same. The relentless, interminable drive of individuals for greater profits, higher wages, higher interest, and greater rents assures that this will be the case. Economists call this process competition. They call its result efficiency. Through this process, inefficient producers, whether workers or entrepreneurs, are driven from the market, leaving behind those who can meet the market test. In Part II, we discussed how this process leads to the intervention of the ruler. Here, I want to discuss another of its implications. This is that in economic life things are never either as good or bad as they seem. This statement was originally made, I understand, by a general who wanted to warn his subordinates of the danger of losing one's head in the press and confusion of battle. But it is also very good advice for someone engaged in the economic process. Since no one really can keep a good thing to himself, you can be absolutely certain that the better your current market position (the greater your current bargaining power) appears to be, the more likely it is that it is being undermined by others as they seek to better themselves. A profitable business attracts competition. A high price for oil stimulates exploration. A trade secret calls forth industrial espionage. All extraordinary rewards are temporary. If they are extraordinarily high, new competition will arise to reduce them. If they are extraordinarily low, the competition will go to greener pastures and they will improve. (There is one important qualification to this last point, however. If the low rewards from a project are due to the use of an inferior technology, there may well be nothing that will improve the situation enough to make it profitable to operate. Consequently, one should recognize the possiblity that even though things may never be as bad as they seem, they can still be pretty bad, no matter how you look at it.)

All right, so things are never either as good or as bad as they seem. What's the relevance of this so far as you are concerned? It is that you should bear it in mind. If, for example, you are contemplating the purchase of a business which has done well in the past, you should not expect it to do as well in the future. You should not enter an occupation simply because it has paid well in the past. Competition will assure that it will not be as rewarding in the future. This point really can't be stressed enough. There exists a whole set of people, for example, who make money by starting new firms, operating them until they become profitable, and then selling them to people too foolish to realize that all good things are brought to an end by competition. Don't become one of those people. Don't ever be led to believe that the value of a business firm can be ascertained by looking at its accounting records. These records may tell how it did in the past. They do **not** tell how it will do in the future. That depends upon what happens in the future, and you must decide for yourself what you think that will be.

To ignore this advice is to risk severe disappointment.

Lesson 19: How to become rich (and what it will cost you to try)

Inasmuch as most of the people who buy and read books such as this one have a secret desire for fabulous wealth (as, indeed, do most of the people who do not buy and read books such as this one), I have decided to include a few instructions in the art of obtaining such.

First of all, you should understand clearly that one does not become rich by working for a salary, by lending money out at interest, or by renting out his land. The reason for this is that no asset will earn more than an ordinary rate of return over the long term. Competition is simply too intense for this to happen. Wages from labor, rent from land, and interest from capital may allow one to live well, but receiving such income streams does not constitute getting rich. Getting rich consists of acquiring the assets which produce these income streams in the first place. How does one do this?

One way to do it, of course, is to save. Saving will result in an increased stock of capital which can then produce an increased stream of interest. But that takes a lot of time and is usually not what one has in mind when he looks for a path to riches. What is the alternative?

It is to be an entrepreneur. To obtain great wealth through your own efforts requires that you either innovate or else speculate. The innovator, as you recall from Part II, gets rich by creating value. He takes a set of productive factors, combines them in some new way so as to produce a product having more value than the factors which went into it, and receives this added value as profit. The speculator, on the other hand, does not create value. Rather, he predicts changes in value which result from economic forces external to himself. "Buy cheap and sell dear" is the motto of the speculator, and he tries to do just that, buying assets which he believes are undervalued in hopes that he can later sell them for more than he paid.

In either case, therefore, whether you choose to innovate or to speculate, the road to riches requires you to become an entrepreneur. In the first case, you must be sufficiently creative to discern the innovative opportunity in the first place and then sufficiently daring to assume the risks involved in seizing it. In the latter case, you must be sufficiently perceptive to assess the future values of assets more accurately than others and then have sufficient faith in your own judgment to gamble your assets on it. Thus, to become rich you must become an entrepreneur. You must detect opportunity, and you must bear risk. You **don't** need to possess a large stock of assets. These can be hired if necessary. What you **do** need is an **insight**, an **idea**, an **opportunity which you discern before the next person.** And then you need the courage to take the plunge. Finally, as we have seen earlier, you need a little luck. The luck and the courage you must furnish yourself. Hopefully, this book will help in recognizing the opportunities which come your way.

What does it cost to become rich? This question is not as silly as it might first appear. Entrepreneurial activity is expensive. It requires time and effort which could be used in other ways. Thus, the cost of potential riches (remember that there is no guarantee that you will actually succeed in obtaining them) is whatever must be foregone in order to free up the time and whatever other assets are required to pursue them.

Lesson 20: It is never too late

In the previous lesson, we discussed what you must do in order to become what was referred to there as "rich," that is, in order to become the possessor of an exceptionally valuable set of assets. We concluded, in essence, that you had to become an entrepreneur. You didn't need a lot of money. You didn't need a lot of land. You didn't need anything, in fact, except an idea, a lot of courage, and a little luck. That conclusion has an implication. It is an implication which I feel justifies a separate lesson all by itself. That implication is that in the economic process it is never too late to improve your situation dramatically.

No matter how old you are, no matter how poor you are, no matter how many times you have failed in the past, you can still get an idea. And if that idea is good enough, it can make you rich.

Lesson 21: Part-timers rarely beat full-timers

Recall our discussion in Part II of the process of creative destruction. This process was described at that time as the one through which firms producing those products least desired by consumers are liquidated during recessions, thus preparing the way for more desirable sets of products in the following booms. While this is correct as far as it goes, there is another aspect of the process which is of interest as well. This is its effect on what might be called the "part-time entrepreneur."

All other things being equal, the earlier in the recovery that an entrepreneur innovates the better (provided, of course, that he does not act before the demand for his product has had sufficient time to recover from the previous recession). Those who innovate early enjoy many advantages. First of all, they are able to obtain the factors of production to build their plants at relatively low prices. Secondly, they are able to borrow the needed funds at relatively low rates of interest. Finally, since they have an early start, their products come on the market early in the boom, and they enjoy the benefit of a long period of prosperity in which to accumulate liquid assets.

Those who come later are in a very different position. Since they are innovating in a period of prosperity, they must build their plants with more expensive factors of production. Since the demand for loans is higher relative to free reserves, they can obtain funds only at higher rates of interest. Finally, since their products do not appear on the market until relatively late in the boom, they must enter the next recession with relatively little financial cushion to carry them through. For such entrepreneurs, reality turns out to be much less attractive than expected, and many, unable to meet their fixed expenses, must sell out at prices reflecting the pessimistic outlook of the recession.

The misfortune befalling such individuals is **not** a random event. It is the natural consequence of their being so slow to innovate and ought to be predictable. Why then do they behave as they do? Why do they first hesitate and then proceed at precisely the wrong time?

They hesitate at first because they lack the courage to proceed. They proceed later on because they make faulty forecasts.

But **why** is this the case?

While not, of course, the only reason, a very major and systematic reason is that they lack adequate capital. Lacking a large capital stock, they are naturally more hesitant to risk losing any given sum. This causes them to hesitate during the highly uncertain stages of the early recovery when they should be going ahead. Lacking sufficient capital to conduct an adequate search for a specialty, they must restrict their attention to an inferior set of alternatives, none of which can be properly evaluated. Lacking sufficient capital to do things right, they must be, as it were, "part-time" entrepreneurs. This causes them first to select mediocre projects and then to proceed with those projects at precisely the wrong time. This, in turn, makes the odds against success extremely heavy, and those who succeed do so largely because of either sheer luck or superhuman effort born of desperation.

The plight of these part-time entrepreneurs is of interest in its own right, but of even greater interest is the fact that it is merely one aspect of a much broader phenomenon which characterizes the economic process. This is the fact that part-timers rarely outperform full-timers.

To see why this is so, just ask yourself who it is that is most likely to own any given capital asset, be it a gold coin or a fast food restaurant. It is that person willing to pay the most to own it. If all individuals have access to the same information and access to funds at the same rate of interest, and if they all utilize that information properly in the decision-making process, then the asset will go to that individual most optimistic about its future.

But who is most likely to be correct about the value of the asset? It is neither the optimist nor the pessimist, but someone in between.

As a result, the nonoptimists are unwilling to pay enough to obtain the asset, and the optimist who does obtain it will very likely have paid too much.

What is required to consistently make money in such a situation? It is superior information. And superior information is only obtained by searching. And who has the time to search? Those with adequate capital.

Thus far we have assumed that all individuals have access to funds at the same rate of interest. This, however, is quite unrealistic. Since those with larger capital stocks can usually provide greater collateral to a lender, they can usually borrow any given sum of money at a lower rate of interest. This means that, all other things being equal, an individual with a larger capital stock would usually outbid an individual with a smaller capital stock and thus obtain the asset. (This statement is based upon the theory of "capital budgeting", a topic of major importance in the field of investment decision-making and a topic well beyond the scope of the present book. Many good textbooks exist in the field of capital budgeting, and I would strongly urge anyone to obtain one and become familiar with its contents before making any major investment decisions. I would also urge them to obtain and become familiar with a good textbook in the field of investments generally. As noted in Lesson 17, the book you are reading is not a book on investing and should not be taken as such.) Hence, in order for an individual with a small capital stock to be willing to pay enough to get the asset he must not only be more optimistic than anyone else about the future of the asset, he must be more optimistic than those with large capital stocks by a margin sufficient to overcome their interest rate advantage. Thus, he must be exceptionally optimistic. Such an individual is extremely likely to pay too much for the asset and, thereby, suffer a loss even if we assume his information is the same as anyone else's.

Lastly, we should note that the individual with a small capital stock is less likely to take the time to really go through the decision-making process properly and, thus, more likely to make costly errors.

Capital is an extremely nice thing to have, and this may suggest to you a reason why the market system is often called capitalism.

Lesson 22: Focus your efforts as much as possible

As should be abundantly clear by now, entrepreneurial success ordinarily requires a great deal of information. Furthermore, it requires it early enough for it to be useful. Now information is only meaningful **in the context of other information**. Consequently, one must **already** possess a reasonable background in an area if he is to be able to rapidly grasp the importance of new bits of information as they come to his attention. Given the constraints under which each of us operates, this requires a rather high degree of specialization in our information-gathering efforts. Very possibly the only way that an individual with average assets can systematically pursue entrepreneurial activity, the only way, that is, that he can reasonably hope to spot a genuine opportunity, is to become as knowledgeable as he possibly can about a single industry.

Lesson 23: Do your own thing

Your stock of assets is unique. There is no one else in exactly your position. This implies that the best way for you to employ those assets is also unique, that is, that it is different from that of any other individual there is. For this reason, you should not try to do what others are doing. They are doing their thing, and you should be doing yours. Specialize in doing those things which are best for you, not in those things which are best for them. The only times you should be concerned about what others are doing are when you think you might be able to copy their techniques or when you think that what they are doing might have a significant affect on the value of what you are doing. In short, do your own thing.

Lesson 24: Don't confuse your occupation with your self

One of the major errors that one can commit in economic life is to lose sight of the fact that he is operating in a dynamic, ever-changing environment, that the outlook for whatever line of production he is currently engaged in will change with time, and that his primary objective in engaging in that line of production is not to produce a specific product per se but to solve his economic problem.

Inasmuch as there is a strong tendency for people to make this error, you should make a conscious effort to avoid it. Don't allow your life as a whole to become too closely attached to the line of production in which you are currently engaged. Select friends who are not associated with your work. Develop interests totally separate from your current line of production. This will make it easier for you to view your specialty objectively, and it will help you to avoid losing sight of a very important fact, namely, that you are engaged in a venture, a venture that could fail at any time, and a venture from which you must be willing to withdraw yourself as rapidly as necessary.

In other words, don't make your specialty the central focus of your life. It is a means of satisfying your desires. It should be viewed as nothing more. If you let it become an end in itself, you are asking for trouble, and you will almost certainly experience severe disappointment as change goes on around you.

Lesson 25: Avoid getting into a bind

In Part II of this book, we discussed the search for a specialty. The point was made there that the shorter the search period, the less favorable the outcome was likely to be. This principle has implications in other contexts as well. One of these implications is that whenever you have something to sell, the less anxious you are to make a deal, the better the price you will be able to obtain. If you are "hungry," if you must sell in a hurry, you will nearly always take a beating. Similarly, whenever you buy something, the less anxious you are to obtain the item, the lower the price at which you will be able to purchase it.

Thus, it is important to foresee your needs as far ahead as possible. This will make you less anxious to close a deal, and will give you the maximum opportunity to make a favorable exchange. Look for a new car, in other words, before the old one fails completely. Sell an asset before you become desperate for cash. Look around for a new job before you actually need one. If you are selling a home, close the deal well before you actually have to move.

Another implication of this principle is that it is always nice to possess some "maneuver area." It is nice, in other words, to possess a sufficient reserve of liquid assets (funds in a savings account, for example) to allow you to make decisions on the basis of underlying values rather than on the basis of liquidity considerations such as how you are going to pay your bills this month. The return on money in the bank can be a great deal more than the interest you receive.

Lesson 26: Live within your means

As has now been indicated a number of times in this book, capital is a valuable thing. And what **is** capital? It is a surplus. It is the surplus of that which is produced over and above that which is consumed. As such, capital comes into existence through the act of saving.

But capital is also something else. Capital is power. It is the power to control your own life. Without it, you are at the mercy of other people. You can be made to do things you detest. You can be driven to a life of crime. You can be put under enough pressure to drive you insane. I can think of no more effective way to maintain your own personal freedom, your personal integrity, and your peace of mind than to build and maintain as large a stock of capital as your own individual circumstances will permit, that is, in other words, to live within your means.

Lesson 27: A good reputation is a valuable thing

If there is one thing that should be absolutely clear by this point, it is that the economic process takes place in the context of uncertainty. We have now discussed a great many implications of this fact, but there is one which we have not touched upon as yet. Furthermore, it is a very important implication. It is that the uncertainty inherent in the economic process puts a great premium upon honesty and integrity. If a man knows he can trust you, he is far more likely to be a buyer of your services than if he does not. He is more likely to hire you. He is more likely to loan you money. He is more likely to buy a house from you. He is more likely to confide in you. In short, you will be able to get more for the things you sell and to pay less for the things you buy if you have a reputation for honesty than if you don't. A good reputation is a very valuable thing.

Lesson 28: The most valuable skill of all

What is the most valuable skill of all? Is there one skill which, more than any other, will help you get the most out of life? I believe that there is. I believe it is the ability to get along well with other people.

The most basic feature of modern economic life is extreme specialization within the division of labor. No one can really accomplish very much of anything entirely by himself. It is the corporation that produces goods, the foundation which does research, the government which wages war. This does not mean that the individual is powerless to produce meaningfully by himself, but how much more effective would he become if he were able to organize and lead a group of people? How much more would he be able to extend his influence and attain his objectives if he were able to work well with other people, to utilize the potential division of labor inherent in any group, to organize and direct their efforts? Aside from the extreme wages paid such exceptional individuals as movie stars and sports figures, the very highest rewards in any economic system go to those who are able to organize and direct large numbers of people for the accomplishment of a given end, to smooth the ruffles which inevitably exist, to keep them moving effectively toward a common goal. To be able to do this is, in my opinion, the most valuable skill that anyone can possess, and you should do your very best to cultivate it if you want the most out of life.

A Final Word

Congratulations! You have now finished what may well be one of the most important books you will ever read.

If you understand its contents, you are a different person than when you began. You are more sophisticated, less gullible, and much more likely to ultimately view your life as a success. As indicated at the outset, economics is not something that one "does". It is something that one understands. If you understand the contents of this book, you will now do the things that you do "do" differently.

If you will now go back and seriously work through the process explained in Part I, you may find that you'll want to do things very differently. **I simply cannot urge you too strongly to do this.** Once you get started, you'll realize what I mean.